The Breadth
of Salvation

The Breadth of Salvation

Rediscovering the Fullness of God's Saving Work

Tom Greggs

Baker Academic

a division of Baker Publishing Group
Grand Rapids, Michigan

Published by Baker Academic
a division of Baker Publishing Group
PO Box 6287, Grand Rapids, MI 49516-6287
www.bakeracademic.com

Printed in the United States of America

Library of Congress Cataloging-in-Publication Data
Names: Greggs, Tom, author.
Title: The breadth of salvation : rediscovering the fullness of God's saving work / Tom
    Greggs.
Description: Grand Rapids, Michigan : Baker Academic, a division of Baker Publishing
    Group, 2020. | Includes bibliographical references and index.
Identifiers: LCCN 2019048616 | ISBN 9781540961952 (paperback)
Subjects: LCSH: Salvation—Christianity.
Classification: LCC BT751.3 .G75 2020 | DDC 234—dc23
LC record available at https://lccn.loc.gov/2019048616

ISBN 978-1-5409-6315-4 (casebound)

20 21 22 23 24 25 26   7 6 5 4 3 2 1

green
press
INITIATIVE

This book is dedicated to the oldest and youngest members of the Greggs family, who are the best of friends, both of whom I love deeply and both of whom bring me countless joys—for my grandmother, Pat, and for her great-grandson and my nephew, Billy.

May you both always swim in the vast sea
of God's saving grace.

Contents

Acknowledgments

This book has been welling up inside me for a long time. It is the best summary I have yet been able to offer of the theology of the gospel of salvation I preach Sunday upon Sunday in little local churches around where I live and have lived. It is the closest thing I can offer to the essence of how I understand salvation. It's not written like my other books in an academic way, but it stems from more than twenty years of theological thinking compressed into what is hopefully a more accessible voice.

I could not have written this book, however, without the profound help and encouragement of others. The first three chapters of this book were given as lectures at Trinity Theological College in Singapore in the summer of 2018. I am indebted to the kindness and hospitality I received at Trinity. My time there was one of the great joys of Christian community in my life. I am particularly grateful to the generosity and grace of all the faculty and staff, especially Mark Chan, Andrew Peh, Roland Chia, Edmund Fong, and Theng Huat.

I was able to complete this book, and to turn talks and lectures into a single volume, because of the kindness and generosity of the H. E. Butt Family Foundation, which allowed me to be scholar and writer in residence at Laity Lodge. I am deeply indebted to

Steven Purcell, who has become a friend, for organizing this opportunity; to the fellowship and hospitality of Jeff and Susie Johnson, Ben Kyle, and Tim Blanks; and to the chefs and cooks who (over) nourished me while I was there—Ryan, David, Luz, Desiree, and Donna—as well as all the other staff who made my time so peaceful and fruitful.

The editors at Baker Academic have been invaluable to the production of this volume. Dave Nelson, Tim West, Ryan Davis, Ann Smith, and Kristie Berglund have all much improved the quality of the book. Any remaining errors are mine and are present despite their best efforts.

That my wife, Heather, allowed me to go on retreat to finish this little book should also be met by intense thanks, as should all of her support, kindness, and understanding in relation to my work and vocation. Most of all, I must acknowledge and give thanks for her unending and unfailing love and care. She has taught me much about the practical realities of living in God's grace.

I came to salvation through my own family—my father, who came to know Christ as Savior when I was a child, and my mother, who also came to live within that reality soon after. Without them and their guidance I would never have come to know the Lord. And it is to the Lord of our salvation that I give my deepest thanks for guiding me throughout my life and for the gift of salvation—the heights, depths, and breadth of which I shall never fully know.

Introduction

There is an old proverb from the Indian subcontinent which (in various forms) tells a story of six blind men who cannot comprehend what an elephant is. They are taken to an elephant in order that they might use their sense of touch to discover what it is. The first is led to the elephant's trunk, and, placing his hand on it, he recoils violently. "An elephant is a type of snake!" he cries. The second is led to the elephant's tusk. Once he places his hand on it, he jumps away. "An elephant has the largest and sharpest teeth in the world, and must devour humans!" The third blind man is led to the tail and, placing his hand on it, says to the others, "I do not know what you are talking about. An elephant is clearly just like a cow—so what is there to be afraid of?" The fourth and fifth are led to the side and leg of the elephant, respectively. The fourth, touching the hard and slightly muddy side of the elephant, declares that an elephant is like a wall, and the fifth, touching its leg, is convinced it is a tree. Finally, the sixth blind man, a brave and patient soul, is taken to the side of the elephant and, placing his hand on it, gently works his way around the majestic creature. "Only when you put all of these parts together," he remarks to his companions, "will you ever understand the whole. This creature is neither snake, nor man-eater, nor cow, nor indeed a wall or tree.

This creature is an elephant, and it is beautiful and unlike anything else I have ever known. Now I know what an elephant is."

When we see only in part, we find it hard to comprehend the whole. We jump to conclusions based on our limited exposure. And when we are not patient to see the whole, we sometimes get things dreadfully and disproportionately wrong. For a long time, in the puzzles section on a Saturday morning, the newspaper I read in the UK used to enlarge a small section of a photograph, and the challenge was to guess what the whole of the object was. It was much harder than one might imagine. Seeing only a part of something out of proportion distorts our imagined sense of what that object is. We fail to see it properly because of the limits placed on our exposure to the whole. We cannot grasp, from the part we see, what the whole is. And our minds confuse the part we see for the whole, limiting that whole to our limited experience.

As Christians, we do this with regard to salvation all the time. We all too often hold too narrow a view of all that God's salvific grace has done for us. We all too often limit the sphere of God's saving act. Our theological imaginations cannot comprehend the majestic mercy of the Lord and all that the Lord has done for us. Our minds cannot grasp what our God has done for us and for the creation God loves. And rather than behold and recognize the overwhelming and blinding light of God's saving work—a light that beats back our gaze—we look so often instead at just one area of the darkness which the light has illuminated, confusing that area of illumination with the light itself.

Yet what right have we ever to limit the friendliness of the holy God toward the creation? What right have we, knowing what God has done for us, ever to place limits on what God does in saving the world God created and loves in merciful grace? Every breath we take, we take because of the Lord's mercy and grace. Every moment that the creation is sustained is because of God's patient reconciling and redeeming desire. Every flap of a butterfly's wings, every blossom of a flower, every spring of water which bubbles over is because God loves and *saves* the creation which God made for God's glory. Isn't that what the story of Noah and the glimpse of every rainbow remind us of? God *saves* and *desires to bring salvation* to the creation. God is the God of salvation, and God is constant and faithful to Godself.[1]

And when we speak of the God who is the God of salvation, we do well to remember that God in God's saving grace is the God of majesty, of glory, of unending plenitude. Just as God's life is one of immeasurable and unimaginable vastness, so too is God's salvation. As creatures within the creation, when we behold and know God, we stand as if we are on one side of a prism, seeing the refracted light in what is to us a spectrum of difference. We describe divine attributes and characteristics as if they were discrete colors that stand almost in contrast to each other. So we think of God as holy, and then as glorious, and then as all-powerful, and then as loving, and so forth. We treat aspects of the divine life as if they were parts, and all too often we are unsure of how they relate to one another. But to do so is spontaneously to fall into some form of polytheism (confusing the attributes of the one God with a manifold pantheon) or the ancient heresy of partialism (dividing God into parts). However, we need to remember at every point that, in the words of the ancient Hebrew prayer, the Lord our God, the Lord is one (Deut. 6:4). God is in Godself that perfect light, and it is only the limitations of our creaturely minds that divide God's attributes like the colors of the spectrum of light through a prism. It is not that we are to think of God as holy, and then as glorious, and then as all-powerful, and then as loving, and so forth. We are to think of God who in holiness is glorious and all-powerful and loving and so forth, and in glory is holy and all-powerful and loving, and so on and so on of all of God's life and ways.

This is true of God's salvation. God is no less majestic, no less glorious, no less all-powerful, no less all-knowing, no less patient, no less loving, no less the God of unending and immeasurable plenitude in salvation than in any other aspect of God's life and ways. A former colleague of mine used to describe to students the unending majesty of God's life in the following way. He would tell them to imagine Monet's *Water Lilies* in the Musée de l'Orangerie. These comprise eight enormous panels depicting the lilies in his water-garden. They cover over two hundred square meters. They are breathtaking, and one can get lost in each one of the enormous panels. If we imagine the scale of this artwork to be God, all of creation across all of time would comprise just one single brushstroke. And all that we could glimpse of God would be the brushstrokes around our own. God's plenitude is beyond all our wildest imaginings. And that is as true of God's salvation as it is of any other of the ways or life of God. After all, God is one.

So often in the life of faith and in the life of the church we fail to grasp the immensity and plenitude of God. And the poverty of our theological imaginations so often can lead us to be the un-rejoicing older brother captured in our sense of our relationship with the Father and unable to see the depth and breadth of the Father's love and mercy toward all his children (Luke 15:25–32). We fail to grasp the intense aliveness of God who is at work in all creation, bringing it to the redemption for which God created it. We place limits on God's desire for the restoration of all things. We do not see the grandeur of all that God is doing to save the creation God loves. We do not understand the magnitude of the great cost that God paid and the lavish riches that this salvation offers in so unbelievably many ways. St. Paul reminds us of the power of God's salvation in those amazing words of unending comfort: "For I am convinced that neither death, nor life, nor angels, nor rulers, nor things present, nor things to come, nor powers, nor height, nor depth, nor anything else in all creation, will be able to separate us from the love of God in Christ Jesus our Lord" (Rom. 8:38–39).

Should this surprise us? Would God, indeed, have paid so great a price if the returns were as impoverished as we so often think? Yes, God would have done all this for just one of us. But there is not just one of us; there is the whole of creation. Yes, God puts us right with Godself. But we live in relation not just to God but to all the creation God has brought into being. Yes, our sin is blotted out. But our lives are also abundantly new.

We need once again—afresh and anew—to be captured by the height and depth and breadth of God's salvation. We need to be inspired once more by all that God has done, is doing, and will do for us. We need to lift our voices once more with Welsh hymn writer William Rees (1802–83), whose hymn "Here Is Love" casts a vision of the unending vastness of saving grace:

> Here is love, vast as the ocean,
> loving-kindness as the flood,
> when the Prince of Life, our Ransom,
> shed for us His precious blood.
> Who His love will not remember?
> Who can cease to sing His praise?
> He can never be forgotten
> throughout heav'n's eternal days.
>
> On the mount of crucifixion
> fountains opened deep and wide;
> through the floodgates of God's mercy
> flowed a vast and gracious tide.
> Grace and love, like mighty rivers,
> poured incessant from above,
> and heav'n's peace and perfect justice
> kissed a guilty world in love.
>
> In Thy truth Thou dost direct me
> by Thy Spirit through Thy Word;
> and Thy grace my need is meeting
> as I trust in Thee, my Lord.

Of Thy fullness Thou art pouring
Thy great love and pow'r on me,
without measure, full and boundless,
drawing out my heart to Thee.[2]

William Rees glimpsed something of the vast enormity of all that God has done for creation in Jesus Christ. He saw the powerful tide of salvation in whose movements we swim. He knew the cost and the power of all that the life, death, and resurrection of Christ achieved for the creation.

The intention of this book is to help us glimpse something more of the breadth of salvation. It seeks to look at the breadth of the ways that we can understand salvation, the breadth of what salvation does in the realities of ordinary creaturely life, the breadth of scope that salvation has, and the breadth of response to the saving grace of God.

1

The Breadth of the Cross

In Liverpool, where I come from originally, there is a restaurant which might sound disgusting but which I love. It is a hot buffet restaurant which serves all kinds of foods—Indian, Chinese, Thai, Italian, British, Mexican, barbecue. Whenever I go, I always feel somewhat disappointed by how boring so many of the other diners are. Some have a little bit of lasagna and a couple of pieces of garlic bread and a salad with Italian dressing. Some are eating just one variety of curry with rice and naan. But this place is a buffet! Its joy is the wide variety of food on offer all at the same time. It is not a place to hold back but a place to feast. And so I like to mix it up a bit: Italian starters, Thai mains, maybe with a couple of sides of Indian food. And there's always space for a few spring rolls, isn't there? After all, what's the point of a buffet like this in its feast-like proportions if you don't feast and feast on, savoring and delighting in all of the variety?

When it comes to the events of saving grace which Scripture records, so often we're like those boring people who can only focus on one thing—who only have one sort of food or one dish at a buffet. We talk about sacrifice, or redemption, or substitution, or atonement, or love, or satisfaction, as if only one image were available, only one understanding were possible. Better, it seems, to be like me at a buffet—and taste everything you possibly can: to feast on God's salvation in Jesus Christ. Why? Because the salvation achieved in Jesus Christ, the richness of the events of his life, passion, and resurrection, offers us a feast for our fallen humanity, which—when it is explored in its depths—teaches us what it means to have the deposit of salvation through the Holy Spirit today. There is a breadth of imagery in the story of salvation, and we should feast on that breadth. Scripture is not a textbook with a formula in it that reduces everything to some great equation in the sky. Scripture is the record of God's saving grace through Jesus Christ—in anticipation in the Old Testament and in recollection in the New.

As a systematic theologian, but most of all as a Christian preacher and as a churchman, I can think of no topic that is more important than the good news of Jesus Christ and of the loving and merciful grace that is the divine origins and ends of his life, death, resurrection, ascension, and return, which is known to us in faith through the self-giving of his Holy Spirit. But we so frequently confuse the person of Jesus Christ and all Christ achieves with our understandings of *how* salvation took place. As Christians, we should never forget that it is not our understanding of salvation which saves us but the Savior himself. He is the good news. He is the one we are to proclaim. He is our origin and our end, the Alpha and the Omega.

Salvation in Christ, Not in Models of Christ's Atonement

Despite the magnitude of this most important message of all time, so often within the church we have reduced the captivating, powerful, life-changing, history-shaping reality of the salvific work of the God of the gospel to reductive, overly conceptualized, semi-contractual, self-limiting models (interpretations and understandings) of the atonement. And we espouse our favorite of these as if there were only one, and—worse still—as if the *model itself and not Jesus Christ in his self-sacrificial life, death, resurrection, and ascension* is the basis of salvation.

What do I mean by this? I mean that when we try to explain and describe the saving work of God, that work of description never takes the place of the God who saves in Jesus Christ by the Spirit. Our accounts of salvation are our best attempts at understanding *all* that God has done for us. They offer us aids and assistance with which to understand something of the breadth and plenitude of the narrative of God's salvation. But sometimes we have considered these explanations, descriptions, and reflections (the models of the atonement) and our knowledge of *them* salvific. We have failed to see that they are not salvific; all they do is point to Christ, who is the Savior. And at times we have used these models as a badge of our Christianity (or our authentic kind of Christianity), claiming that only we (and those who agree with us) have the right knowledge of how salvation works, and therefore we alone are saved.

So we talk sometimes as if substitutionary atonement as a concept, or satisfaction as a model, or participation in Christ as a theological formula were the saving thing. But they are not. Salvation comes from Jesus Christ himself in obedience to the Father's saving will and known to us through the Holy Spirit's saving presence in our lives. All that these reflections and models do is to try to understand that reality more deeply and to grasp components and aspects of Scripture in what it tells us about our salvation. Furthermore, when we place so much emphasis on the one model or understanding of salvation we like and look to, we limit the breadth of the images and models of salvation God offers us in Scripture and the capacity these have variously to capture our theological imaginations. And even then, with our focus on our preferred model, we limit so often what we think the effects of salvation are—accounting only for the activity of God in putting us right with Godself, not considering the breadth of what God does, and failing to attend to the simultaneous restoration of our relationships on the horizontal plane both within the church and within the world. And still, it seems to me, we operate with our judgments about salvation as if *we* were those who judge between the sheep and the goats, as if *we* were able to see as God sees—to see the heart. We limit the breadth of God's salvific reach and its inherent surprises to those who are like us, enacting that unholy puritanical judgmentalism that says, "Only me and thee are saved, and I am not so sure about thee." And how we identify those who might be saved is through identifying a *response* to faith similar to our own. Only those who have repented in a certain way, or prayed the Jesus prayer, or are able to narrate the exact moment of conversion, or can speak of the sacramental journey through baptism and confirmation—only those who accord to our own mode of response to salvation—are those whom we see as authentic beneficiaries of all that God has done in saving grace.

Now, before people get overly anxious about what on earth it is that I am saying, let me be clear about what I am not saying. I am *not* saying that interpretations and models of the atonement are unhelpful or unnecessary. I am *not* saying there might not be some understandings and models that more helpfully indicate the narrative of Scripture than do others, or that it might not be through a particular one that we view the others. I am *not* saying that salvation does not concern the reconciliation of God and humanity in the person and work of Jesus Christ (quite the contrary!). I am *not* saying that faith in the gospel is unimportant or that a response to God's grace is not profoundly important. And I am most firmly *not* saying that some unlovely principle of universality can be applied in any kind of way that undermines the urgency of the gospel and the reality of divine judgment.

What I *am* saying is this: salvation is only in Christ, only through grace, only by faith (*solus Christus, sola gratia, sola fidei*, as the Reformers would have it). We must put the *person* of Christ and the grace of the God of the gospel and the beautiful breadth of

Scripture's account of this grace which we know in faith back at the heart of our accounts of salvation. We do well to broaden our minds to the vast horizons of salvation of that particular life, death, resurrection, and ascension of Christ for creation. So, rather than reducing our accounts of Christ's salvific life and work to some essence captured in an overly formulized and one-dimensional model, interpretation, understanding, or concept, in all our speech about salvation we must point back to and describe the contours of the saving life, work, and person of the Savior Jesus Christ, through whom alone salvation comes. We need to be open to Scripture's richness and breadth. We need to put the Saving One right at the heart of our accounts of salvation.

And this will interrupt us and wake us from our lazy and narrow views of the God of the gospel. Indeed, any discussion of salvation that we undertake should seek to proclaim the *interruptive* event of God's reconciling grace in Jesus Christ—an event that continues to interrupt us, raise us from our comfort, even in the life of faith. At the center of our understanding should be the Christ who is known by the Spirit—the human life, death, and resurrection of the person who is perfectly obedient to the Father and who, as the incarnate God-human, mediates God's grace perfectly to humanity. All too often, our attempts at describing and understanding the concrete drama of God's reconciling grace fall prey to a mechanized overconceptualization, such that the human Jesus is eclipsed. The life and humanity and narrative of Jesus known in the Gospels is subsumed to some kind of conceptual framework. This understanding moves beyond the level of description to the point where the understanding itself is considered to save. So, we are saved by substitutionary atonement, or by the satisfaction of God's honor, or by justification, or by the victory of redemption. To this kind of understanding we must say: No! We are saved by the God of salvation, the God of the gospel, the God who is known to us supremely in Jesus Christ by the Spirit. Jesus Christ is not the outworking of some understanding or model of salvation: Jesus Christ is our salvation! All that models or interpretations can do is to point to him. He is not an illustration of them; they are an illustration of him.

The focus on single models and understandings of salvation with such heightened importance runs deeply contrary to classical, creedal Christianity. Technically speaking, there is no dogma (no absolute, agreed theological statement by the church) of the atonement as there is of the Trinity or of the person of Jesus Christ. The ecumenical councils never settled—nor found it necessary to consider—which model or understanding of the atonement was *the* model or *the* understanding to which all Christians should adhere. Instead, the Nicene-Constantinopolitan Creed (of 381) *narrates* the broad contours of the life of Jesus (the salvific *events* of his life) in the context of the gracious incarnating of God's Son in creation:

> For us and for our salvation
>> he came down from heaven:
> by the power of the Holy Spirit
>> he became incarnate from the Virgin Mary,
>> and was made man.
> For our sake he was crucified under Pontius Pilate;
>> he suffered death and was buried.
>> On the third day he rose again
>>> in accordance with the Scriptures;
>> he ascended into heaven
>>> and is seated at the right hand of the Father.
> He will come again in glory to judge the living and the dead,
>> and his kingdom will have no end.[1]

The Council of Chalcedon (in 451) added greater reflection on the dogma of Christ's *person*: Jesus Christ is *one* person (Jesus Christ) in *two* natures (God and human)—the hypostatic union of God and humanity in the one person Jesus Christ. Chalcedon, like the previous councils, also states that the Son of God's becoming human is "for our salvation." But it never enshrined a conceptual model in relation to the *work of salvation*. What am I saying in pointing to this? I am saying this: when we confuse the effect of the saving events of Christ's life, death, and resurrection with adherence to a particular conceptual model, interpretation, or understanding as a shibboleth that ensures our salvation, we not only part company with classical, creedal Christianity; we eclipse Jesus himself, the acknowledgment of whose lordship and resurrection brings to us the benefits of the reconciliation of creation which he brought about through his incarnation, life, death, resurrection, and ascension. But does this mean that interpretations and understandings of salvation have no place? Does it mean we do not need to love God with our minds when we meditate on God's saving grace? Not at all.

So What Do Theologies of the Atonement Do?

The very best interpretations and understandings of the atonement are those which effectively paraphrase the atoning life and work of Christ, known to us in Scripture, and point us *back* to the biblical text and its language and—crucially—to the interruptive encounter with the one about whom that language is concerned. In short, the very best accounts of salvation make plain through their focus on Scripture that salvation comes *only in and through Christ*.

John Calvin's great theological work, *Institutes of the Christian Religion*, does just this. In book 2, paragraph 16, Calvin, with light but profound conceptuality, follows through the narrative arc of the creed, using this as the means to reflect on the biblical account of the saving life, death, resurrection, and ascension of Jesus. In chapter 17, there is a more conceptual set of reflections around the concept of substitutionary atonement and Christ as the price of human redemption (see below), but again with a profound sense of the testimony of Scripture to the saving life and acts of Jesus Christ. Indeed, for all of the seemingly speculative and abstract nature of the discussion, even Thomas Aquinas's *Summa Theologiae* follows a similar pattern, structuring the reflections on the shape of the creed and the gospel narrative of the death, resurrection, and ascension of Christ (see III.46–59). These are two of the greatest, most famous, most influential theologians ever to live, and they realized this: theologies of salvation are at their best when they lead us back to the Saving One. They are at their best not when they are overmechanized and overconceptualized but when they follow the pattern of the creed and the gospel—that is, the pattern of the life of Jesus—and point to him. Beyond that, they help to accent the various accounts and images of the life and work of Jesus in Scripture.

We live today in an age in which it seems like two options are available with regard to the broader public outside the church (and, worryingly, sometimes within the church) in relation to the cross. On the one hand, there is the sense in which we have inoculated ourselves to the reality of the event of the cross. We have taken away from it the scandalizing and shocking nature of the story (1 Cor. 1:23). We have turned the cross instead into an item of decorative jewelry, or we have covered the cross with flowers as I have seen repeatedly in churches of late (with no story of the narrative of getting to that point). I am sure we have all heard stories of people going into jewelry shops and asking for a cross, only to be presented with one to which the shopper (who really wanted a crucifix and not a cross) replies, "No, I didn't want one like that. I wanted one with a little man on it." We have lost all sense of the story of the crucifixion—of the costly reality of all that God has done for us.

But equally, on the other hand, we focus so much on the brutality of the cross that we psychologize the brutal and torturous punishment. We do this to such a degree that we focus not on the good news of salvation but on the pain of the event in a guilt-inducing reflection which turns us away from saving grace and back on ourselves, our sin, and our guilt. We see this in everything from certain medieval, mystical meditations on the blood of Christ to nineteenth-century pietistic hymns and their focus on the blood. In popular culture, Mel Gibson's film *The Passion of the Christ*, with its focus on the death of Christ without any context of his life, achieved much the same effect. Although the realism of the gore and blood did much to save the cross from its saccharine imagery, the divorce of the death of Christ (in all its brutality) from his life also fails to recognize the full depths of Christ's crucifixion. Such focus almost turns the death of Christ into an animal sacrifice: the person, his morality, the relationships he had, and the life he lived come to have little significance and are rent asunder from his death. We divorce the events of the passion, crucifixion, death, and resurrection of Christ from the full significance of the incarnation of the Son of God and the perfect, sanctifying obedience of the life of the human Jesus of Nazareth.

In short, both approaches to the cross eclipse Jesus Christ. They make him either a nice man whose life we follow because it makes us feel warm and fuzzy, some cultural-historical-social memory, a bit like the piece of decorative art we hang around our necks, an object of our guilt and sin; or a brutalized and tortured piece of meat without any deep sense of the profound depths of who this one who is crucified is. We need never to forget: this one who in obedience died this horrific death is the Lord of all the universe through whom all things were made (John 1:3) and is the incarnate, eternal Son coequal to the Father.

This same propensity is also found in the degree to which we have displaced the particularity of the *person* and the *events* of the atonement with particular conceptual interpretations, understandings, and models. We have become so attached to particular conceptual understandings that we think that acknowledging the model or interpretation is the basis for receiving the effects of salvation—not that they exist to point us back to the one in whom, when we acknowledge he is Lord and have faith in his resurrection, we are saved. And crucially, we impoverish our sense of the profound depth and breadth of that salvation when we overfocus on one type of imagery, one model, one interpretation or understanding. *The very kaleidoscopic range* of the biblical images of salvation on which these interpretations and models are based offers us a glimpse into the breadth of God's purposes and grace in salvation. But in themselves the images, models, understandings, and concepts of salvation are insufficient corporately (never mind individually) to capture the magnitude, breadth, and intensity of God's saving grace in Jesus Christ.

The Range of Images in Scripture

Any reflection on Scripture must rise to a sense of the breadth of imagery of salvation. We need to try—as best as possible this side of the heaven-and-earth divide—to capture something of *all* that God has done for God's creation in its fallenness. That Scripture does not consistently use only one image of God's reconciling, saving, and redeeming grace in salvation is in itself significant for our reflections on salvation. The breadth of biblical imagery cannot be reduced to one single conceptual model, interpretation, or formula. Let us look to some of these images to gain a sense of their overwhelming variety and breadth.

Redemption

Chief among the images of salvation in Scripture is that of redemption. This is the term that is generally used to render the Hebrew *padah* and *ga'al* (Pss. 74:2; 77:15). These are translated as *apolytrosis* in the Greek of the Septuagint (the Greek translation of the Hebrew Bible), and this is the term also used in the New Testament. Redemption is most often associated with the idea of purchase, of buying back; it is a term still used today in a pawnshop when the customer pawns a precious item to the owner of the shop and can buy back the item for a redemption fee. The imagery associated with this understanding in the Bible is closely related to the account of God's saving work in the exodus: through the Passover, a costly act, the Hebrew people are redeemed from bondage to a new status of freedom and liberation (e.g., Deut. 7:8; 9:26).

But how are we to understand this in terms of Christian salvation today? Of course, there is the question of who or what it is that we are purchased back from. Are we bought back from God's wrath at our sinfulness? Or from the very sin itself and the bondage it incurs? Or from the personification of sin and the agency and rule of the devil? All of these are possible or included in Scripture. And then there is the question of how we are purchased. This is perhaps easier to settle in Scripture: clearly there is a great cost which is paid—a cost we know as we read the story of Christ's passion. This is the cost of *all* that God does for us on earth in God's Son—everything from the hurt of an illegitimate birth, to being outcast, to suffering humiliation, to the cross and its torturous death. Related to this is the question of who it is that redeems us. Here we would surely want to say that God is the agent of our redemption supremely in God's own incarnate self-giving in Jesus Christ. But stopping at this point does not go far enough. There remains the question, To what are we redeemed? We are redeemed to a new status, to the status of adopted children of God, or to the status of those who now belong not to sin and death and the devil but to the God who has purchased us as God's own, to the status of an heir to the kingdom of heaven. Even just redemption alone as an image uncovers a breadth of aspects to God's saving grace in our lives.

However, we cannot stop here. This breadth of images and understandings associated with the idea of redemption alone does not fully capture the meaning to which the idea of redemption points. Indeed, the Hebrew word *ga'al* has a resonance that we sometimes miss. It involves undertaking the part of a kinsperson in saving: if we are redeemed in this sense, we get out of trouble crucially through the action of a member of *our own family* who, for example, pays off a debt. When used in regard to redemption in Christ, this word indicates that Christ undertakes this action as a near kinsperson—as one of us, as our brother, as the one who is *human* as well as divine, as the one who takes our place, as the one who loves us as his own family, his own people. In other words, redemption as an image seeks to capture something of the incarnate Christ: it points back to him in whom alone salvation takes place. It points to him who is the Word who became flesh and dwelt among us, full of grace and truth.

Peace through a Savior and Mediator

Another aspect of the language of salvation is the very word *salvation* or *peace—hoshia* or *shalom.* We find this concept throughout Scripture, especially in the book of Judges (e.g., 3:7–11). This peace, this salvation, is the end of a cycle that is repeated throughout the Hebrew Bible: Israel does wrong; God is angry; Israel is sold into the hands of enemies; Israel cries out to the Lord; God raises a savior; through the savior's acts, Israel now has *shalom* (peace, prosperity, salvation).

The agents of salvation, whether they be judges, kings, or prophets, serve as mediators between God and humanity. Moses himself, indeed, mediates with God and says that if God is willing to forgive Israel, Moses is prepared to be blotted out of God's book (Exod. 32:31–34). He is prepared to be damned himself for the sake of the Hebrew people he loves. Moses displays a two-directional mediatorial saving life: Godward in sympathy with God, and humanward in sympathy with humans. There is an ascent on the part of the human: Moses climbs up the mountain to meet with God. But there is also a descent on the part of God: God descends to meet with Moses in the cloud. Indeed, this idea of salvation through a mediator is at the very heart of the Reformers' advocacy of justification by grace through faith in Paul's theology. For all that this interpretation of Paul is now highly disputed (not least in the reminder many scholars have given us to the focus on the significance of righteousness in Paul), for the Reformers of the sixteenth century the mediating work of God as God-human in the one person of Jesus Christ is at the core of their accounts of salvation and what it means for Christ to die *for us*. It is worthy of note that "for" is in general the rendering of the word *hyper* in the Greek, and that *hyper* (even taking account of the different Greek cases with which it is used) is almost as broad in its meaning as the English word *for*. The exception to this form of the phrase is in 1 Timothy, where the Greek term *anti* (which means "instead of") is used.

But what does it mean to say that Jesus dies "for" (*hyper*) us? Looking at the word *hyper* in context helps, and it also reveals the breadth of meaning. So, for example, in Romans 5:8–10 Paul writes, "But God proves his love for us in that while we still were sinners Christ died for us. Much more surely then, now that we have been justified by his blood, we will be saved through him from the wrath of God. For if while we were enemies, we were reconciled to God through the death of his Son, much more surely, having been reconciled, will we be saved by his life." Thus, in verse 8 we are told that Christ died "for us." This is explained in verse 9 in more forensic language: we are justified by his blood (with its potential ideas of sacrifice) and saved from God's wrath. In this way, there is some sense of the "courtroom" context, which tends (in Protestant soteriologies at least) to unfold in a declarative interpretation of the saving event. But in verse 10 this imagery is augmented and supplemented with a more personal account: we are reconciled to God and now saved by *life*, which means the account is no longer just forensic, since it is life (and seemingly our relationship to that life) and not blood that saves.

Sacrifice

This idea of salvific mediation also gives rise to the idea of salvation through sacrifice. This is a theme not only in the redolent imagery in the Gospels, as they speak of Christ against the background of the temple, but also in Paul (Rom. 3:21–26; Gal. 3:13; 2 Cor. 5:21). Perhaps we see this language most powerfully in Romans 3:21–26:

> But now, apart from law, the righteousness of God has been disclosed, and is attested by the law and the prophets, the righteousness of God through faith in Jesus Christ for all who believe. For there is no distinction, since all have sinned and fall short of the glory of God; they are now justified by his grace as a gift, through the redemption that is in Christ Jesus, whom God put forward as a sacrifice of atonement by his blood, effective through faith. He did this to show his righteousness, because in his divine forbearance he had passed over the sins previously committed; it was to prove at the present time that he himself is righteous and that he justifies the one who has faith in Jesus.

In this account there is a stacking up of imagery and themes and concepts to help us understand what this sacrifice means. Even in the account of Jesus's death as a sacrifice, there is a compounding of conceptual imagery to help explain this—image upon image, symbol upon symbol, theme upon theme. Let's look at these in turn.

First, we must consider the ideas of *righteousness* and *justification*. These two English terms are used to translate a set of Greek words sharing a single stem, which is indicative of the symbiotic relationality of these two concepts. In justification the sinner is made righteous, put right, approved. This idea, as the new perspective on Paul (associated with scholars such as N. T. Wright and James Dunn)[2] has made clear, finds its roots not primarily in classical Greek traditions of accounts of moral integrity but in the Old Testament, and particularly its Greek translation in the Septuagint. The justifying of the human (v. 24) is connected to God's own righteousness (vv. 21, 22, and 25), as verse 26 makes explicit. Righteousness is, in other words, God's saving activity—something that God does in God's covenantal grace.

Indeed, second, this conceptual centrality of grace focuses this justifying activity of the righteous God back onto God, who is the one who takes the initiative for salvation. The work of Christ is the work of the whole Godhead (Father, Son, and Holy Spirit), who desires the salvation of the creation. Grace is the source of the salvation of humanity, and it is because God *already* loves humanity that Christ comes. The source of salvation is the free gift of God in God's grace (God's unmerited, absolute loving-kindness), made effective in faith (vv. 24–25). Grace, we might say, is the root of Christ's saving work rather than just the fruit of Christ's saving work (cf. Rom. 5:8).

Third, sacrifice is explained in relation to redemption (discussed above). But in this passage there is no idea of a *price* being paid by anyone to anyone. What seems more the case is that, through the life, death, and resurrection of Christ, God has rescued God's people in a way similar to God's rescuing the Hebrews from slavery. It is a costly thing for God to do in God's mercy, but God does this in Christ because God desires in love and grace to save and atone and reconcile fallen humanity.

A similar issue arises, fourth, when we probe more into the idea of the *sacrifice of atonement* (the Greek word *hilastērion*). This word has tended to be translated either as "propitiation" or as "expiation." Propitiation entails the idea of the action that one undertakes to appease someone who is angry. When we translate the word *hilastērion* this way, we give a translation that follows the meaning of the word in classical Greek. In this account Jesus's death appeases the divine wrath through God's own self-giving in the death of the incarnate Christ. This view certainly takes the gravity of sin seriously. But the great New Testament scholar C. H. Dodd argued in 1936 that it is better to render *hilastērion*, when it is used in the Greek of the New Testament and the Septuagint, as "expiation."[3] In this sense, the word tries to capture something of the impersonal setting right of wrong since God cannot be seen to appease Godself. In the Septuagint, God is almost always the subject of the action applied: God is the one expiating. God puts wrongs right. The argument goes that ideas of wrath and anger could presume a division in God's person and a failure for us to understand God as constant, faithful, and one; and so it is better to translate the word *hilastērion* as "expiation." And yet, even these two options do not capture everything since the word *hilastērion* is used in the Septuagint to refer to the mercy seat—the lid of the ark of the covenant. Here, pointing back to the incarnation, it is not only the case that Jesus's blood is sprinkled, but also the case that Jesus as the God-human (fully divine, fully human, and one person) is the very place where the blood with its atoning sacrifice is sprinkled. This, once again, is an attempt to capture the reality that his person and work are inseparable.

Fifth, salvation through sacrifice is expressed in terms of God showing God's righteousness by passing over sins (v. 25). Here again, righteousness is God's saving activity. God saves by (*dia*) passing over sins. What we see here is a positive statement in personal terms rather than an abstract notion of God fulfilling some kind of divine law of justice: this is God's saving activity *now* in the forgiving of the sin of the people. There is covenantal language in use here (recalling the Passover and God's righteousness) which now applies to all people who have faith and not just those who are included in the covenant through the sign of circumcision (cf. 1 Cor. 5:7; 11:25–26).

Salvation from Sin

This final point leads us to reflect a little more on how salvation is salvation from sin: Christ's atoning work not only reconciles us as creatures to God but reconciles us as *fallen* and *sinful* creatures. Again, multiple images are used in discussing the overcoming of sin. Paul speaks of Christ as the *last Adam* (1 Cor. 15:45; cf. Rom. 5:12–20).

Christ reverses the sin that comes into the world through Adam, and now—rather than belonging to sin—we belong to Christ. Alongside this is a sense of freedom from bondage. Jewish thought contemporary with the writings of St. Paul spoke of evil angelic rulers as rulers of nations. Paul adopts these ideas but applies them to structural evil—the very way the world is. Apocalyptic theology (associated with people such as my colleague Phil Ziegler)[4] has returned our attention to this. Rulers and principalities and powers are those things over which as individuals we have no control and from which only Christ can set us free. This involves not only Satan but also powers that are bigger than any individual human and to which we are subject.

Paul also uses forensic language to describe Christ's work of setting us free from sin. This involves the wrath of God in response to human sin (Rom. 1:18–31; 8:1–39) and the idea of propitiation (discussed above). It is worth remembering that wrath is potentially not ultimately negative: wrath is not the opposite of love; indifference is. A parent who loves her child does not let her do just anything, and the parent's anger is aimed at the betterment of the child. Moreover, these accounts of divine wrath and judgment are given *because we are saved from them*; they are not an ultimate description of our condition but at best a penultimate description. Again, this connects with our understanding of the word *hilastērion* and what it means to say that Christ died for (*hyper*) us. "For us" might mean (as it does for Calvin) "in our place" by way of substitution, or it might mean "as our representative" or "by means of identification." Or it could be that all of these ideas are in operation. For example, Christ substitutes for us in our place, and Christ is in his resurrection the representative of what we might be: because he is alive, so are we.

In Christ

A further way to conceptualize this work of salvation has to do with the language of being in Christ (*en Christō*) in Pauline terms, or to dwell in Christ in more Johannine terms. Christians *share in* or *participate in* or *are united in* or *abide in* the action and person of Jesus by being "in Christ" (Rom. 6:1–14). A lot of ink has been spilled on this language (not least from my own pen). Put simply, the participatory language of being in Christ, sharing in his humanity, is a reminder that Jesus's death is inseparable from his life: it is his life, death, and resurrection as a whole that saves (cf. Phil. 2; Rom. 5); it is in his body that we are brought to the Father. We share in his humanity and become human in him. We find our life in him.

So What Is the Point of All This?

Where does the overwhelming complexity of these pictures leave us? In little more than a tangled mess, it might seem. But to stop at this point is to fail both to love God with our minds (as we are called to) in thinking about what this might mean and how this might be interpreted today, and to understand Scripture as a living, divine address to humanity through the Spirit. Although what has been said already in this section may seem complex, it is only the tip of the iceberg. The array of imagery in Scripture to explain the breadth of God's salvific purposes is best understood as a deep nexus of roots from which the tree of life grows forth with all its branches and leaves. Rather than assuming confusion or even contradiction, we must try to understand the complementarity of the wide variety of images expressing the magnitude of what God has done for us. It is a little like looking at the Sistine Chapel. All the parts are beautiful in themselves, and when we focus in on individual aspects, we find it difficult to relate them to the whole. But were we to lie down on the floor, look up, and gaze on the whole ceiling, we would see the nexus of images and be overwhelmed by its complexity and beauty—not trying to understand all its parts, as there is too much and that can only happen when focusing in on one section or another, but instead beholding its magnificence.

Scripture, as we have seen, uses a variety of images in its description of salvation. Just within Paul's letters, no single image dominates. Even within Scripture, therefore, reflections on the salvific meaning of the life, death, resurrection, and ascension of Christ present themselves as just that—reflections on a reality. They are in themselves already descriptions of the reality of salvation that the earliest church believed it had received from Christ's life and death. Not even the Bible saves; the Bible proclaims the Saving One and points us to him. When the writers of the New Testament were inspired to write, they were in their own times already offering interpretations and understandings of the events surrounding the life and death of Jesus. In doing so, they depended not only on the narrative of those events, which ultimately came from the apostles, but also on the concrete reality of them—the reality of what they meant for them in their own lives of faith.

In Scripture, the depth of the reality of who Christ is and what Christ has done for us is captured with the piling of symbol upon symbol, image upon image, picture upon picture, interpretation upon interpretation, in a way that is meant to overwhelm us with all that God has done for us. This breadth does not mean that we necessarily have to see all of them in equal order: one image can be used to interpret another, or as the lens through which we read others; or certain images might be more helpful for certain people at certain times, or help to make sense of the reality of what Christ has done for certain cultures. But we can never claim that there is just one image and stay true to the Word of God. The images are manifold because the blessings of salvation are manifold.

The Breadth of Models or Interpretations of Salvation

It is this attempt at trying cohesively to hear and understand the gospel and communicate it to people that motivates the activity of arranging the scriptural material into models, understandings, conceptualizations, and interpretations of the atonement. These are attempts at expressing core (or the core) realities of Scripture's portrayal of the benefits of Christ's life and passion. These models and interpretations point us in helpful ways to themes which exist in the scriptural testimony—themes that are helpful in the proclamation of the good news of salvation, themes that point us to all that God has done for us in Christ. Order is important here and should determine the status these models hold. These are *reflections on the reflections* that already exist in the scriptural testimonies of the gospel narrative, for the testimonies themselves already reflect on the incarnation of the one Word of God, whose life, death, and resurrection are so significant that we are told there are not enough books in all the world to contain them.

Models of the atonement attempt to speak to the needs of people in given cultures and times and inevitably *accentuate* particular aspects of the Bible's reflection on Christ's life and work. But what they can never do is *supplant* the biblical witness, reducing its pouring of symbol upon symbol upon symbol to attempt to grasp in creaturely language all that God has done to the level of a single, exclusive essence. And we can never presuppose that it is the articulation of the right model, not the one to whom the model points, that is the cause of salvation.

Satisfaction

This tendency to overemphasize a model of the atonement is perhaps most pronounced with the satisfaction model, which often becomes a badge of evangelical theology (my own tradition)—a little bit like the cross on one's lapel, the WWJD wristband, or the fish bumper sticker on a car. All too often, for all its help in bringing us to understand aspects (perhaps even the primary aspect) of salvation, the model has functioned in such a way as almost to presume that it is the articulation of satisfaction as a theory of atonement that brings about the very benefits of salvation. The satisfaction of

God's honor appeals especially to Romans 3:26 ("It was to prove at the present time that he himself is righteous and that he justifies the one who has faith in Jesus") and brings about an objective approach to the description of salvation. Salvation, in other words, is about what was done for us once and for all.

Most famously associated with the medieval theologian Anselm, the model helpfully coheres with his view of Christ as true God and true human in one person.[5] Anselm's work is an excellent reminder of the incapacity to separate the passion of Christ from the life of Jesus and the incarnation of the Son of God. For Anselm, the atonement is a matter that concerns God in Godself; it is objectively something God does, and does not simply concern the attitudes or behaviors of human persons. Redemption comes both from divine grace and through Christ's voluntary obedience. God in Godself does what is—and this is a crucial term—"fitting." This fitting action is salvation's response to sin. Sin, for Anselm, is interpreted as not rendering "what is due" to God, and it would not be "fitting" for this failure to render what is due to God to go unchecked without remedy. For God to do nothing about this would be for God to fail to uphold God's own justice. Therefore, God acts in justice to maintain God's own "worth" in dignity; that is, who God is demands that sin cannot be ignored when it happens. To ignore sin would undermine both God's justice and God's honor, as God's justice means sin has to be acknowledged and accounted for, and God's honor would be lost unless punishment or payment occurs to rectify the situation. But a loss of God's honor can only be rectified by God. No human can return to God the honor God has lost. And yet this would not be a human offering were it not a human who offered the satisfaction of God's honor. Therefore, as our substitute, Christ, as God and human in one person, dies for our sins. As Anselm argues, no one but God can make the satisfaction, but it would not be humankind's satisfaction unless it were by a human; therefore, satisfaction of God for humanity can only be made by the God-human, the incarnate Jesus Christ, who does in our place what we cannot do.

Crucially, for all the significance of this account, it trades on medieval feudal structures in its explanation: it is modeled on the failure of a peasant to render the honor (to make the feudal payment) that is due to the overlord whose land the peasant farms. The account is, for all its power and correspondence to the biblical witness, itself a *contextual explanation* of the saving work of Christ for the age. It trades on an *illustration* in order to make the biblical images of the passion of Christ meaningful for those to whom the gospel is proclaimed. In short, it is an account developed to help the proclamation of the gospel to the age in which Anselm wrote. It is akin to the use of contemporary music in modern worship songs—a contextualizing of the gospel to the context in which it is proclaimed in order that people can understand it and come to know the Lord to whom it points. This is not to say that Anselm's imagery and explanation of salvation have no power now; quite the contrary is true. But it is to say that, for Anselm, his model and understanding of salvation never had the status of unquestionable authority and dogma. They were ways for him as a preacher to preach the good news so that people would understand it in his setting.

Penal Substitution

Such an objective account of salvation became particularly significant in the Reformation with its emphasis on penal substitution. The account of honor in Anselm is redefined less in terms of the contextual language of "rendering honor" and more in terms of the biblical language of grace, faith, and righteousness. For the Reformers, the cross becomes central to the way they explain and understand salvation. As Luther states in the Heidelberg Disputation (1519), "He deserves to be called a theologian . . . who comprehends the visible and manifest things of God seen through suffering and the cross" (thesis 20).[6] A theology of the cross (*theologia crucis*) becomes everything. Christ on the cross takes our place, is our substitute: Christ dies *instead of us*, and our sin is laid on him (Isa. 53:6). Salvation comes only through faith in this. As the Schmalkald Articles of 1537 remind us, "Jesus Christ, our God and Lord, 'was handed over to death for our trespasses and was raised for our justification' (Rom. 4[:25])."[7] Salvation cannot come, therefore, from any place but comes only from the grace of God in Jesus Christ, a grace which is known by faith. As Luther wrote in his *Preface to the Epistle to the Romans* (1522), "Faith is a living, daring confidence in God's grace, so sure and certain that a person would stake his life on it a thousand times."[8] This faith alone gives access by grace alone to Christ, by whose death alone we are saved.

Victory

Although many accounts of salvation focus on Christ's passion and death, Gustaf Aulén has reminded us of the centrality of *victory* as a model for understanding salvation.[9] This is a trope which he says is core to the Bible's message and to understandings of salvation throughout the history of the church. In Christ's victory, humanity is redeemed *from* jeopardy *by* a costly act *to* a new state of being (as we have already seen in the account of redemption). The victory trope is evident in the parable of the strong man bound by a stronger man, and picks up the Old Testament stories and expectations of the warrior-leader and their associations with Christ (Isa. 59; Ezek. 34). The Old Testament themes of conflict develop into notions of conflict with sin, death, and the devil. This theme, for Aulén, is also present throughout the patristic era. Irenaeus's (ca. 130–200) account of salvation involves Christ reversing the fall by triumphing over temptation through his obedience to the Father. Irenaeus uses the idea of recapitulation as a way of describing the reversal of the creature's lot through Jesus's triumphant victory over the devil. This victory comes ultimately through the death of

Christ but also through Christ's life, in which he experiences what
sinful humans do but does not fall prey to the temptation to sin.
For Irenaeus, therefore, the temptation of Christ has a profoundly
salvific aspect, as in this we can have victory over sinful temptation:
Christ overcomes the sin Adam fell prey to, reversing the effects
of the fall.

Moral Accounts

All the models discussed so far are highly objective in form:
they concern what God does and only what we do insomuch as
we put faith in that objective work. But alongside these accounts
have been more subjective, human accounts—moral interpretations which focus on the teaching of Christ and our apprehension
of that teaching in our lives. Most famous is the account of Peter
Abelard (1079–1142),[10] which is focused on the divine love known
in Jesus Christ; but in more modern times Friedrich Schleiermacher
(1768–1834) and Albrecht Ritschl (1822–89) in different ways also
offer us moral conceptualizations of the atonement.[11] Drawing on
Romans 3:26, Abelard argues that Christ rescues us from false own-
ership and "by word and example . . . [has] bound us to Himself by
His love."[12] Christ's passion and death show forth the love of God
for us (Rom. 5:5–6; John 15:13). There are moral effects of Christ's
death through seeing, receiving, and replicating this love, and these
accounts point us back to the significance of understanding Christ's
death in the broader contours of his life. In a postmodern era with
its appeal to "nonobjective" thought, such accounts have proved
popular, even if they cannot capture all of the aspects of Christ's
saving work; moreover, in failing to see the objective work of God's
salvation in Christ, they potentially fall prey to an Ebionite Chris-
tology (which sees Christ only as a human moral teacher and not
as God). What these moral accounts do, however, is point us back
to the very narrative of Jesus's life and passion; they bring us back
to Christ, through whom alone we are saved.

Multiple Models and Interpretations

These models in their very differences pick up and accentuate themes that we find in the Bible about the meaning of salvation. Their value and worth are not found in the exclusive focus on any one of them. Their value is found in the capacity they have to speak into the contexts in which they are written. The church received a contextual interpretation from Anselm. It was reminded by the Reformers, in an age of complex ecclesiastical rituals, of the simple saving message of Jesus Christ and him crucified. Other models reminded the church of the significance of the whole life of Christ for the victory over sin in the forms it takes in every age; or they acknowledged the need for Christ to be not just one with whom we have some kind of contractual relationship but one who is our example and the image of our humanity. In all these cases, the models arose *from* the texts of Scripture and the explanations within it, highlighting aspects of the vast and beautiful vista of salvation Scripture describes to us. And in the end, the models point us back to the events of the act of God in the saving life, death, and resurrection of Jesus.

The Breadth of the Human Jesus's Passion

The story of the concrete events of the incarnation, life, passion, death, and resurrection of Jesus are the core of our salvation. Moving beyond these and their narration and seeking to make sense of the concrete events of salvation too quickly runs the danger of moving past or eclipsing Christ. We need to remember that our models, interpretations, and explanations—however helpful—are intended to aid understanding as we seek to love God with our minds, and to lead us back to Christ, through whom and in whom alone salvation takes place. We cannot too quickly offer an explanation of salvation in such a way that we move past the real human history and the real human pain of Christ, or else we will turn salvation into a formula and instrumentalize Christ to that formula: Jesus becomes not the one who is our salvation but a component in some cosmic equation. Whatever we do with our reflections on the events of Christ's final days and resurrection, we cannot move past the gospel and the very history, the very story, of the events of Christ's passion. Instead, until we know as we are known, we must hold our explanations lightly, as they are aimed at humbly leading us back to him and the events of his life, death, and resurrection.

If it seems like I am over-egging the pudding, I hope I will be forgiven. But I think it is necessary. One reason I think this is that I always ask students the question, Why did Jesus die? I get all kinds of answers, often in the language of biblical imagery or else in the language of one or other of the models of the atonement. No student has ever answered that Jesus died because people (men!) killed him. In trying to make sense of it all, we rush past the very human events of the final week of Jesus's life. We do so to such an extent that we even forget that Jesus died because people killed him! Imagine for a moment reading this story for the first time—without any sense of the ending or the broader context. Surely, we would be struck by how little sense this story makes. Here is a man who has done no end of good—who has healed the sick, liberated those who have been captive, fed the hungry, offered wise and wonderful teaching, included the outsider, never put a foot wrong in his relationship with the Father. He enters Jerusalem and is hailed as the Messiah. And then, within just a few days, the crowd is baying for his blood, and he hangs there dead. There is a senselessness to the narrative of the gospel which is, as Paul tells us, foolish and scandalizing. However much we interpret and explain Christ's death, there is always an element in the human story that—before we aim to make sense of it—we must acknowledge does not make sense as a narrative.

Let us think about those final days and hours, and the human emotion and interactions in them. In Gethsemane, Jesus says, "My soul is overwhelmed with sorrow to the point of death" (Mark 14:34

NIV). All things, we are told, are possible for the Father—even to prevent Jesus from having to endure the cross. But God wills this horrific end for him in order to save humanity, and Jesus submits to that will (Mark 14:35–36). And we will never fully understand or capture what that means, but we will glimpse something of the cost of it. Even in submitting to the Father's will for us, Jesus, we are told, is overwhelmed with sorrow to the point of death.

In his sorrow, in his being overwhelmed, we find a human story. And that human story meets us at the place where we need salvation—at the point of our sorrow, our trouble, our grief, our fear, our death. We find salvation in Christ when we are overwhelmed; and through the incarnation, God is fully, completely present there in our humanity through Christ's. When we rush to meaning, when we rush past this story, we do not see the depth and breadth of the benefits of our salvation: the benefits of being met by our God, to whom salvation belongs, in our points of need; the benefits of being met by the man Jesus, being met by the one who says to us in our trouble, "I am here. I too have been troubled in my soul even to the point of death." When we move past the scandalizing, seemingly senseless aspects of the story to an explanation or interpretation or model, we miss the breadth of salvation's power.

Similarly, we are told that Jesus in his greatest hour of need is left alone and everyone deserts him (Mark 14:50–52). Jesus's sense of loneliness is brought about by being the worst kind of stigmatized outcast. He is now a person whom others—even his closest friends, who have promised to be with him to the end—don't want to be with: "Then *everyone* deserted him and fled" (Mark 14:50 NIV). There was surely never such loneliness as there was for the one who gave himself over entirely for others: knowing that he was about to do this for all of creation and yet deserted by all of humanity and alone; willing as the Son of God for all eternity to do this for human beings but finding not one human being who would remain with him through it.

When we feel that there is no one in the world who understands us, when we feel alone, when we feel stigmatized, or outcast, or friendless, let down by those around us we love—then and there the salvation of Christ finds us. Then and there, we can cling to the cross of Christ, where *alone* the Son of God—whose very being is a communion with the Father and the Holy Spirit—is deserted and lonely as he gives himself over for all creation. Our God is not just with us when we are lonely; God is with us in sharing our loneliness and understanding, in empathizing with our condition. In Christ we have one who suffered the most profound loneliness for us because he is our true and unfailing friend. A concept or a model can never teach us this.

The same is true in relation to the humiliation of Jesus at the hands of the soldiers (Mark 15:16–20). Our God, who is the great I AM, has no ego whatsoever. When we hear of Jesus being humiliated and mocked, when the soldiers put a purple robe and a crown of thorns on him to humiliate him, when they hail him as the king of the Jews, they get it wrong. They get it wrong not only because he *is* the king of the Jews but also because he is so much more than that. For this man that they spat at and struck, mocked and cursed, is not only the king of the Jews and the Son of David to be hailed. He is also more profoundly the High King of Heaven. He is the ruler of the whole universe. He is the Lord of all creation. He is the God of gods and the Lord of lords and the King of kings. He is the God who is so holy that Moses could only see his back, and even still Moses's face shone with the radiance of God—the God who is so holy that only once a year could the high priest enter the holy of holies. Every breath we take is an act of his grace. And yet he is humble enough not to turn around and exclaim with all the thunder of the heavens to the mocking soldiers the wrath of the Almighty to rain down lightning bolts on their heads. He has grace and forbearance in his humility, which meets the pride of our sin. Here is salvation: here in him and his passion.

I could go on with so many examples. What does it mean, for example, for Jesus to die crying out to God in doubt, "My God, my God, why have you forsaken me?" (Mark 15:34). It means he finds us in our own sense of forsakenness. Or what are we to make of the complexity of human interactions we see around the cross and with the body? There are complex, salvific interactions with the women who stand faithfully at the foot of the cross; with the faithfulness of Joseph of Arimathea, who asks for the body and buries it; in the grief of Jesus's mother and of Mary Magdalene; and in the sorrow and failure of all the disciples, especially Peter. These all tell us of the human realities of God's salvation, which meets us in different situations and places of our lives.

In the seemingly senseless aspects of this story, in the human suffering and pain of the Christ who has done no wrong, who has healed and forgiven and included and liberated and brought good news, there is foolishness and a scandal. But in this is the concrete mercy of God's saving grace as it meets us in our places of need. When we consider the narrative reflections of the Gospels, we can never move so quickly to explanation that the passion and cross cease to be a stumbling block. We should not so rush to explanation that we skip over the events of Christ's passion and even Christ himself, through whom alone salvation comes. In this story, there is a point of contact between God and us in our pain and loneliness and struggle and sorrow. In this, we learn in our woundedness to say, "By his wounds I am healed" (cf. 1 Pet. 2:24). We are met by salvation in the breadth of our moments and places of need. In them, we see something of the vast breadth of God's salvation.

Conclusion

Does this mean that we give up on explanations of the atonement, or that we simply stop with the narrative of the concrete events? Does it imply that we cannot explain why Christ died and how salvation happens? No, not at all. In Scripture and the tradition of the church we are given a rich feast of imagery, symbolism, explanation, and human emotion and interaction. We are to enjoy that feast, to feast on the plenitude of the vast, capacious, generous saving activity of God's goodness to us in Jesus Christ, which cannot be captured in or reduced to any single image or model. If we reduce the whole of Christ's life, passion, resurrection, and ascension to some overly mechanistic formula in which it is only a contributory part; if we focus exclusively on the mechanics of atonement; if we talk about *just* sacrifice, or substitution, or victory, or forgiveness, then we will miss the vast richness of salvation in the events of God's grace.

It's like dining at that buffet I described at the start of this chapter: better to make the most of it, to take all kinds of parts of the imagery that feed our souls, than to monotonously eat just one thing. God gives us a feast from which to have foretastes of the heavenly kingdom, in which we will sit down and feast with the saints in the light of the presence of the Savior of all.

2

The Breadth of Salvation in the Society of God

One of my great struggles and disappointments in life is our apparent incapacity as human beings to consider the needs and concerns of the other in our daily living. This is something which genuinely depresses me. I come across this all the time, not least in my travels. People will barge past you in the queue (which is sacrilege for a British person!) in order to get on the train or bus or plane first—either to grab a seat or to store their luggage. And they do so with their heads down, ignoring everyone else—and this in spite of the fact that they have just broken three ankles with a trolley bag and sent an old lady toppling! And it's exactly the same getting off. Indeed, I sometimes think that miracles actually take place at the airport, as those who need help boarding a plane often enough are able to rush off after landing and take down anyone who stands in their way as they exit! As humans, we find it very difficult to look beyond ourselves—our own needs, our own desires, our own wants, our own rights, our own experiences. And we often are unconcerned about how this might affect other people. Indeed, we valorize it in calling it the virtue of self-assertiveness.

That self-assertiveness easily can become a means of justification for selfish behavior. I find it so upsetting that (at least in the UK) people cannot simply say "sorry" any longer—beyond the foppishly British way we all do within polite conversation, that is. If you point out that a shop or a bank or a company or your employer or a colleague has done something wrong (something which might have hurt you or caused you to be inconvenienced), you do not get an apology but an explanation (a justification) for why this happened—often with the caveat that this does not in any way indicate liability. When we do get apologies, they are often unhuman announcements from machines at airports or railway stations which do not unconditionally apologize but—again—explain why the delay has happened and apologize for any inconvenience that *may* have been caused, and not what *has* been caused. Or else they are extremely limited—the worst being an apology "that you feel that way." In our relations with each other, we prioritize ourselves, our sense of ego, our rights and wants over everyone else. And we do so all the time.

I am sure that I am as culpable of this as anyone. We believe ourselves to be the center of our own universe. But we are not: God is the center of God's own creation, of the whole universe; and when we realize that, we come to see that our own egos need to fade away significantly. But to do that, we need saving grace.

What is most worrying for me is that we replicate this kind of self-oriented behavior in the church. We are so concerned in the church to focus on the salvation of the individual that we sometimes fail to see that we need to be rescued from this type of behavior by God's salvation, and indeed sometimes the very way we frame our accounts of salvation contributes to this self-obsession. Our hymns speak of "*my* Savior" and "*my* salvation" all the time. We focus on the individual relationship we have with God. And none of that is wrong per se. It is wrong, however, if we fail to see that calling Jesus "my Savior" means that we can no longer live like we exist in isolated bubbles of our own selfish desires.

It is said of the earliest Christians that people knew they were Christian by their love. Indeed, the very Savior that we proclaim to be "mine" and with whom we seek to have a "personal" relationship is the very Savior who tells us we will find him in the poor and the needy and the naked and the homeless. He is the Savior who tells us that whatever we do to the least of his brethren we do also unto him. He is the Savior who reminds us not only to love God with everything we have but also to love our neighbor as ourselves. He is the Savior who challenges and broadens our concept of brotherliness and of neighborliness. He is the Savior to whom we seek to conform in taking on his likeness. He is the Savior who not only opens the path to heaven but changes the nature of the world *now*. He is the Savior who reconciles us with God and—in his own body—with one another as well.

Accounting for the vast number of images, explanations, understandings, and stories of salvation in Scripture and the teaching of the church is only the first step in seeking to understand the breadth of salvation. There are not only broad descriptions of salvation but also broad *effects* of salvation—some of which we often overlook. One such aspect of salvation is that God does not just save us from sin and death for eternal life with God, but that in salvation we also *already* anticipate eternal life. One underdeveloped aspect of the breadth of salvation that God brings about, we might say, is the salvation of God in the society of God. This is the saving effects of God in the life of the church—how the creation of the church offers us salvific possibilities through the work of the Spirit.

Christ's work of salvation through the Holy Spirit puts us right with each other in the horizontal axis of creaturely existence as well as putting us right with God in the vertical. Crucially here, the one axis does not come at the expense of the other, but *both* are aspects of the very breadth of salvation. This is a concern that I have had for a long time, and it is the basis for a much larger project of mine on the church, called *Dogmatic Ecclesiology*.[1] God puts us right with one another as well as with Godself. We are creatures who live in time and space, and the gospel calls us to a new life in that context—to the freedom to love unconditionally just as Christ has loved us. What is more, this loving of one another is part of the breadth of salvation. Let us begin this account by looking at the very origins of the fallenness of humanity.

A Vertical and Horizontal Fall

The Origins of Sin

Sin arises from humanity's breaking its relationship with God through disobedience. Adam and Eve disobey the one command God gives to them in the context of God's superabundant grace in creation: they eat the forbidden fruit. But the immediate consequence and effect of this act, even before the description of the rupture in the relationship with God that follows, is a pronounced awareness of *individualism* as a primary identity. Adam and Eve no longer are who they are in relationship but are who they are in their alterity to both God and each other. Their individualism is accompanied by a sense of strangeness in regard to the other, a relationship of fear toward the other, and actions of blame of the other in comparison to the self. St. Augustine and Martin Luther have both famously taught us that sin causes the heart to turn in on itself; we become consumed with ourselves, who we are, what our rights are, what we have. This means our relationship with God is broken, as we look to ourselves (wanting to know ourselves what right and wrong is, wanting to be our own "gods") and not to the Lord. But this turning of our hearts in on themselves in sin alters not only the relationship with God but also the relationship with other humans and the creation.

Sin is the prioritization of the self, we might say, over divine *and created* others. Having eaten the fruit, the man and woman understand themselves to be naked in front of each other and cover themselves, aware and ashamed of their difference (Gen. 3:7). Their difference is understood not primarily in terms of intimate relationality but in terms of distinction and otherness. Furthermore, having hidden himself from God because of his nakedness when God walks in the garden, Adam immediately seeks to divert blame away from himself and toward Eve, and indeed through this to God. He blames "the woman whom [God] gave to be with [him]" for eating the fruit (Gen. 3:12). Adam is (wrongly and self-justifyingly) clear that this fruit was given by Eve and God. Rather than protect and care for and love this one whom God has given him—this one who is his other half—he offers her up to protect himself. The fault, according to Adam, cannot be his: preservation of his individual self over against the other (even the most intimate other) transcends unity and co-humanity and relationship to God who gives all things. The woman then also redirects blame away from herself toward the serpent (Gen. 3:13), again trying to preserve herself rather than ask for forgiveness and love.

Acceptance of the self's wrongs and desire for forgiveness are lost at the cost of preserving the self-perceived (and perverted) justice to which one feels individually entitled. And this comes to stand in a series of competitive relationships—competition between humans, humans and God, and humans and the creation. In short, we see disjointed and conflictual individual reality arising immediately from the fall, with the first glimpse of a sense of separate and individualized identities not only in relation to God but also in relation to other humans and the rest of creation (which is now at enmity with the human).

Relationships outside of Grace

As soon as the human being yields to the temptation to step outside that relationship of grace, she ceases to participate in the

grace that allows her to be oriented toward another (whether divine or creaturely) and not herself. Outside grace, humanity finds
itself without the ability to receive and share in God's absolute, free
loving-kindness. This affects proportionately the human being's
orientation toward those around her in the horizontal plane of
creaturely existence. That Genesis records that it is one individual
who is tempted to behave thus, and then the other also partakes
of the forbidden fruit, further underlines the degree to which the
individual's self-awareness and self-orientation are key. This is a long
way from the origins of man and woman recorded in the second
creation story:

> This at last is bone of my bones
>   and flesh of my flesh;
> this one shall be called Woman,
>   for out of Man this one was taken. (Gen. 2:23)

The unity and sense of identity between man and woman in the
second story (emphasized by the rib taken from Adam) indicates
that a turning toward the other (indeed a co-humanity) was originally a (perhaps the) central feature of the creation of humanity.
This is also evident in the first creation story, in which the unity of
man and woman is linked with being made in the image of God:

> So God created humankind in his image,
>   in the image of God he created them;
>   male and female he created them. (Gen. 1:27)

Male and female are created together, and their joint creation is in
the image of the gracious Creator. There is no individualism here,
and human unity ("them") is related to the image of God, who in
creation gives Godself to be for another. In the story of the fall,
it is the person's *individual* identity in relation to another (both

God and another human being) that begins to define what a fallen human looks like.

Human nature is corrupted by sin. Sin alters the relationship that exists not only between the human person and God but also between human beings themselves. Sin's effects are not only vertical but simultaneously horizontal. Because humanity no longer seeks to be oriented toward God and to share in the good gifts of God's grace, the human shifts the focus of her orientation onto herself. There is an awareness of individual identity in a relationship of (potentially conflictual or hostile) alterity toward *both* God *and* other human beings. Indeed, to be aware of other options beyond immediate obedience is itself to be aware of oneself over against God. No longer are one's actions determined by a shared co-willing with God, but one has a distinctive will aside from God's will. What is more, these broken and now hostile and competitive relationships open a Pandora's box. As soon as one person protects her identity, another jumps to do the same. Egos are challenged and bruised by egos. Hearts turned in on themselves compete for the biggest share, for the self-justified existence, for domination, for self-preservation at the expense of another. As Gandhi so famously described, the problem with "an eye for an eye" is that eventually all the world will become blind. We exercise our own justice and sense of rights, and who we are as individuals in ourselves (rather than in relation to God and one another) becomes the be-all and end-all.

The Need for Saving Grace in Reconciling
Our Human Relations

Overcoming this situation of sin and its effects requires divine salvific grace. Humans in their fallen condition always tend, not toward love of other in sharing in the eternal loving of the Father and Son in the Holy Spirit or the overflowing love of God in grace toward that which is not God, but toward the self-preservation of the individual. It is an act of the grace of God for the human to be able to be oriented toward another—both God and other human beings. Indeed, in this the human participates in God's grace toward the creation and the Son's being loved eternally by the Father. In other words, to be able to live in love with one's neighbor, in peace in the world, in relationships of trust and grace and self-giving, requires God's salvation. As humans we have screwed this up, and only God's salvation can put it right. We need God's saving grace as much for this as we do to be put right with God in the first place.

Accounts, therefore, of the restoration of creation from the fall require an account of the operation of God's act in restoring the relations of humans to other humans as well as humanity's relation to the rest of creation, since these horizontal effects, too, are consequences of fallenness, along with broken relations vertically between God and the human. The divine gift of community in the church, through an act of the Spirit, is a reversing by grace of the fall and its effects.

Christocentric Horizontal Reconciliation

Christ's Work of Restoring Our Relationships with Each Other

In general, accounts of salvation focus on the work of God in the incarnation of the Second Person of the Trinity, God the Son, the Lord Jesus Christ. Salvation, as we all know and are told, comes through the God-human, Jesus Christ, who mediates God to humanity and humanity to God. The key concern here is that the fall is overcome and humanity is offered salvation by restoring the relationship between God and humanity. Humans are saved by the grace of God in Jesus, who, while we were still sinners, died for us (Rom. 5:8). For us and for our salvation, God became human, as the creed attests. It is only as a gift of God's grace that humans are saved, and God's merciful, free loving-kindness is such that God chooses not to be without the fallen human creature.

For God, however, horizontal and vertical sin (sin against other humans and creation, and sin against God) cannot be differentiated.

All sin is a falling short of God's glory, and it is only (as we have established) by participating in the good grace of God that any human can share in being oriented away from the self and toward the other in creation. This horizontal reorientation of humanity in which hearts are turned out to the other in creation is no less a work of God's salvation than the vertical restoration. And both occur at once: there is no communion with God without communion with one another, and there is no true communion with one another without communion with God.

This is no new discovery. Often this point has been made in relation to the work of God in Jesus Christ—through a moral example, through Christ's command, through Christ's discipling, or through participation in Christ's humanity. And all of this is true. As fallen humans, we desire to "be like God": *that* is the temptation the serpent offers to us. We fall through our rejection of our creatureliness, of our humanity. So, in the work of salvation, God becomes human to teach us once more what it means to be human. Indeed, there is a danger in the way we speak of salvation, when salvation comes to be about escaping our creaturely realities and ineptly copying what belongs to the divine: it becomes all about my capacity to put on "ruby slippers" in heaven, so to speak—all about the otherworldly. We respond to God's saving grace by once more wanting to be like God rather than accepting our gracious status as creatures of the Creator. We invert all that God has done for us in Christ, and—rather than realizing he left the glories of heaven to become human for our salvation—we try not to be conformed to his likeness as a human but to ignore our creaturehood and to focus on heaven alone. We want to be like God. To save us from this, Jesus becomes human. We need to learn the salvific grace of becoming human, becoming creatures, once more—not try to escape to another (heavenly) realm.

Dangers for the Church in This Approach

But we encounter a potential problem here. If Christ's work of salvation is one of teaching us how to be human, there is a danger that our act of seeking to become human in following Christ is understood or enacted as a human work rather than an action of divine grace. In other words, we think we can become disciples of Christ unaided by God's grace. We think we can live lives in the image of the humanity of Christ by following his example in our own efforts. Put in classical theological terms, when we focus on the pedagogical activity of Christ in helping to make us human, we sometimes fall prey to a Pelagian understanding of salvation. Pelagianism was a heresy of the early church which said that we receive salvation and live holy lives simply by an exercise of the will, through which, indeed, we are able to live like Christ. It was a puritanical movement in which there was no room for grace, and in which salvation came to the human unaided by divine grace and simply by following Christ's example. In our relationship with other humans in salvation, just as in our relationship with God in salvation, we cannot be saved unaided. We need grace. We need God's absolute and life-transforming loving-kindness. We need God.

Attending to the full breadth of divine salvation helps here. Attending to the work of the Holy Spirit's grace offers us a means to realize the effects of divine salvation in the horizontal axis of divine salvation. The Holy Spirit is at work in our lives, establishing not only communion between us and God but also communion among humans in the society of God.

"To Your Advantage That I Go Away": The Breadth of the Spirit's Work of Salvation

Attending to the Spirit's Saving Grace

The work of the Spirit in establishing the life of the church and in putting right our relationships with one another can fall into the background of our accounts of salvation. We too often focus on "me" and "my relationship with God," failing to realize that when we do not love those around us, we do not know God (1 John 4:7). And we do not account sufficiently for the grace of God's Spirit in bringing forth that love as a fruit of the salvation that God brings about.

Yet the teaching of Jesus is that it is *better* that he should go so that that another Paraclete should come (John 16:7; cf. 14:16). Perspectives that underplay the Spirit's work in salvation narrow accounts of God's salvation, and this has a profound impact on the way we describe horizontal dimensions of salvation. Indeed, it has a profound impact on our accounts of the Christian life, often reducing the human-to-human relations negatively to a merely natural or self-willed activity. We don't see the full breadth of what God did, does, and is doing by God's Spirit in reconciling us not only to Godself but to one another in creation. There is a need for the horizontal work of God's salvation to be considered more fully, and for a broader account of the continuing work of salvation which the Spirit is undertaking in the time between the ascension of Christ and his return. This is the time of the patience of God; it is the time of God's work of reconciling us to one another; it is the time of the church. God's work of sanctifying us (making us holy in conforming us to Christ Jesus) is a salvific act that reverses the effects of the fall by returning humans to communion, not only with God in Christ, but simultaneously with each other through the saving work of the Holy Spirit.

The Spirit's Work of Inbreaking the Future into the Present

This reversal of the fall's effects is a reality that Christ has achieved for us through the cross and the sending of the Spirit. But this objective reality, this thing that God has done, is also something that God is doing now in the world by the Holy Spirit. And the first concrete context of this (the first fruits of this salvation) can be found in the event of the Spirit's act in establishing the church in the horizontal plane of human existence. The church is an *event* of the Spirit's act; that is, it is not the sum totality of the act of the Spirit since the Spirit blows where the Spirit wills and is extensively present in and to the creation. But the event of establishing the church is an intensive work of the Spirit; the establishing of the church in which there is now to be no division, since we are one in Jesus Christ, is a continuing work of God's salvation before Christ's return. It should be an anticipation (ahead of time) of the kingdom of God. The Spirit's work in this is one of inbreaking into the present in creation from God's future. In this proleptic inbreaking of the future in time, the Spirit establishes restored and redeemed interhuman relations. These new restored relations redefine the identity of the fallen human who is being reconciled and redeemed. In salvation, the creature becomes one who no longer has her heart turned in on itself in self-preserving and self-justifying egoism. Instead, through the Spirit's saving grace, she is free—free to be one whose heart is being turned outward toward God and simultaneously outward toward the other in creation.

The place in which this turning outward should begin is the life of the church, because through the Spirit in salvation we discover ourselves as within the corporate body of Christ, in which the individual finds her primary and most basic identity. In a church in which we do not choose our fellow worshipers, we find a community of given others in their differences—differences of race and class and education and opinion and age and social standing and wealth. And these others are to be to us fellow members of the body of Christ, fellow heirs to the kingdom of God, fellow children of the Father of all. They are to be to us objects of brotherly and sisterly love, not because we might gain anything from them, nor even because we might enjoy their company or find in them people who resonate with us, but because they are given to us as those to whom the Spirit turns out our hearts in love as the Spirit turns out our hearts in worship of God. In being caught up with the Spirit's movement with, in, and to the creature and the Spirit's work of relating salvation to the creature, the creature is herself moved in the movements of the Spirit's grace, and moves on the horizontal axis of creaturely existence toward the other whom God also loves.

Becoming Truly Human through the Spirit's Salvation

We become human, therefore, in the salvific grace of God in Christ through the Holy Spirit's indwelling of us. But we do not change in our being in this action; this is not a transformation away from being creatures or a lessening of the absolute difference that exists between creatures and the Creator. We don't replicate Adam and Eve's desire to be like God. Rather, participating in God's saving grace, we become actively more human. This becoming more human happens as the indwelling of the Spirit grows and grows within our lives. We become not *less* creaturely but *more* creaturely; our humanity is increased, deepened, reconciled, and made whole again as God eternally desired. As those who are filled with the Spirit, we become the creatures we were always meant to be and we become the creatures God created us as before the fall. We become creatures in the likeness of the one through whom all things were made. We come to share in his humanity. And this happens as, through the indwelling of the Spirit, we share in the humanity of Christ, on whom the Spirit rested fully and intensely. We often think of Christ as sharing in our humanity. I am not sure that quite captures it. His is the perfect humanity; his is the eternal humanity in whose image we are made. He is the true human, and we are not yet truly human.

To be wholly and truly human is to live in salvation in Christ, and to live in salvation in Christ is to be wholly and truly open to the filling of the Spirit of God and the event of the Spirit's grace. To become more human and to increase our humanity is to be completely open to and drenched in the Holy Spirit. The more the Spirit dwells with us, the more human we may become. Why? Because the more we receive the Holy Spirit, the more we are conformed to

Christ as the perfect and true human who was in his life totally and utterly filled with the Spirit of God. The more we participate in his Spirit-filled humanity, the more we become the perfect humanity of his body. The Roman Catholic theologian Yves Congar elegantly puts the matter thus:

> The Spirit, who made the humanity of Jesus . . . a completed human-ity of the Son of God (through his resurrection and glorification, Rom. 1:4; Eph. 1:20–22; Heb. 5:5), does the same with us, who are of the flesh from the moment of our birth, and makes us sons of God, sons in the Son and called to inherit with him and to say after him: "Abba, Father" (Rom. 8:14–17).[2]

The Spirit's perfect presence in the life of Christ is what it means to speak of the perfect humanity of Christ in which we are called in salvation to share. This is a humanity in Christ which, through the Spirit's self-effacing grace, is oriented toward the Father who loves the world and toward the world which is loved by the Father.

Since the creation that exists in time and space is the condition in which created humanity exists, in time and space Jesus's humanity flourishes to be the complete and perfect humanity. The true hu-manity we behold in him is the humanity in which all humans were determined to share and into which, in the body of Christ, we are formed. The descent of the Spirit onto Jesus at his baptism is the realization in time and completion of his true humanity; this is in part why the baptismal narrative follows the infancy narratives so closely. Christ's is a life of utter dependence on the Spirit as the one who is conceived by the Spirit, the one on whom the Spirit descends at the baptism, the one who is led out into the wilderness by the Spirit, the one whose ministry takes place as the one on whom the anointing of the Spirit rests, and the one who in his resurrection breathes his Spirit. His human life on earth in space and time is a life perfectly filled and a ministry completely led and governed by the

Spirit. Yet Jesus is not only the one who is baptized and receives the Holy Spirit; he is also the one who baptizes with the Holy Spirit (cf. Mark 1:8). He immerses those who follow him with the same Spirit who rested on him fully so that they too may in salvation share in him, in his perfect and true Spirit-filled humanity.

St. Paul picks up this link between Adam's creation, Jesus's baptism, and the giving of the Spirit when he writes, "Thus it is written, 'The first man, Adam, became a living being'; the last Adam became a life-giving spirit" (1 Cor. 15:45). By receiving the Spirit of God, we become more and more truly human because, by an event of the saving work of the Holy Spirit who dwells within us, we too come to share in the perfect, Spirit-drenched humanity of Christ. In this, in more formal theological terms, we are freed to participate both passively (by the objective reality of God's grace in salvation in all that God has done for us) and actively (through our creaturely acts and behaviors that correspond to that saving reality) in Christ's full humanity. Second Corinthians 5:17–18 captures something of this: "So if anyone is in Christ, there is a new creation: everything old has passed away; see, everything has become new! All this is from God, who reconciled us to himself through Christ, and has given us the ministry of reconciliation." God has done something for us in which we are passive: there *is* a new creation; the old *has passed* away; everything *has become* new; God *has reconciled* us to Godself in Christ. But there is also a new life that is active—the ministry of reconciliation. In sharing in God's reconciling grace in Christ, our humanity is reconciled and we become reconcilers with one another. This is the new creation; this is the true humanity.

This true humanity is a humanity that participates in Christ and therefore has an identity more foundational than any individual identity each human may possess (hence the body imagery in Scripture). Clearly, Jesus's is a life that shares fully (uniquely) in God's life through the unique event of the incarnation. God has become, in the Second Person of the Trinity, this *particular human*, Jesus. But by the saving work of the Spirit, we too share in Jesus's humanity. The same Holy Spirit who breathed life into humanity and rested fully on Christ is intensely present to his people, dwelling within them and working within them, conforming them into the likeness of Christ. We share in Christ's humanity to such a degree, indeed, that we are enabled to become adopted children of God (Eph. 1:5).

In sharing in this perfect humanity of Christ by the indwelling of the Spirit, broken human-to-human relationships on the horizontal plane of existence are restored in salvation as humans are able to participate in the grace of God (vertically) and, in this participation in Christ, are oriented away from themselves and outward toward others. Indeed, this "outward movement" toward others is the foundational nature of God's grace, as God wills to be *for another* in creation—even in its fallen state. This reorientation of humanity and restoration of human-to-human relationality is a saving event. It is an act of the Spirit of God, who makes us participants in the body of Christ. In Christ, we not only share in his mediating work between God and humans, but we also recover, by the Spirit, what it means to be fully human as God eternally determined humanity to be. This true humanity involves participating in God's grace through restored vertical relations to God, and so thereby to be turned away from ourselves and our inward-turned heart and turned outward toward others in our horizontal relations within creation. By being a member of the body of Christ, our humanity becomes the humanity it was created by God to be—humanity in the form of Christ, who is the one completely and perfectly filled with the Spirit and the one in whom we participate.

True Humanity as Co-humanity

This is a co-humanity rather than an individualistic humanity—a humanity whereby we do not exist by ourselves or even in groups or organizations that gather together as individuals, but in which we *share in one another*. As Paul puts it in Romans, "So we, who are many, are one body in Christ, and individually we are members one of another" (Rom. 12:5)—very different from the lapsed humanity that expresses itself in the heart turned in on itself.

In the first instance, the context in which sharing in this humanity is possible is the church as a place in which the gospel is proclaimed and in which there is also a givenness of the other as a gift of God in the creation. Of course, we all know that there continues to be sin and fallenness in the life of the church. No one who has ever experienced the church could ever deny that. And as the old saying goes, if we ever did find a "perfect" church, we should never join it as we'd only ruin it! The church is not the kingdom of God; it is not fully redeemed; it is still part of fallen creation which is justified in Christ. But the church is an *anticipation* of the saving and redeeming grace of God, who seeks to put right our relations with one another.

Indeed, other people in the church become essential for the identity we might have as participants in the body of Christ. The body imagery is not of individual "Christs" who create themselves to be images of Jesus. Instead, the image is of corporate life in which the parts are meaningful only in relation to the whole, and in which the whole, the (singular) body of Christ, is the most significant aspect of our identity as those saved by grace. Sharing in the body of Christ is a participation in the true humanity, since it is a participation in the co-humanity we share in Christ by the Spirit, who frees us to be ordered toward God and neighbor. It is in this humanity that we are presented to the Father, and also in this humanity that we can discover and know what the other's personhood means for us as a defining feature of who we are at our most fundamental level. Dietrich Bonhoeffer, the great theologian and martyr of the twentieth century, raises this issue well:

> For only through the person of Christ can the existence of human beings be encountered, placed into truth, and transposed into a new

manner of existence. But as the person of Christ has been revealed in the community of faith, the existence of human beings can be encountered only through the community of faith. It is from the person of Christ that every other person first acquires for other human beings the character of personhood.[3]

Only as we know the other in Christ do we encounter them truly as they are. And only in Christ are we freed to live toward and for the other. The image of the body of Christ reminds us that the community is only united as it exists in Christ by the Spirit and is aware of the mutual interdependence of the members of the community. The Spirit frees us to live for others and, in so doing, to live actively as a part of Christ's body. To be filled with the Spirit and thereby to share in the true humanity of Christ in salvation is to be opened up toward the other and to see one's own identity as bound with the other in Christ at a more fundamental level than individual identities. The other whom we encounter in the church in all its breadth is essential to this primary identity we have in Christ.

Salvation through Loving the Given Other

Moving in the Movements of Grace

The work of the Spirit, therefore, is one which makes known and present to the horizontal axis of creaturely life the reconciling and redeeming act and works of God on the vertical axis in the reality of ordinary createdness. This work involves catching us in the ways of salvific grace now as we are being reconciled and redeemed from our fallen, sinful state. In bringing the unique, one-off work of Christ's salvation to the context and contingency of everyday life with its ordinary interactions, the Spirit does not impart a "fact" or a piece of knowledge or an additional characteristic or a set of teaching. Rather, the Spirit captures the creature up into the Spirit's own way, allowing the believer by the Spirit's saving work to participate in the divine way of grace. This way of grace is a way which freely flows from the inexhaustible and complete life of God toward the creation—that is, toward that which is not God. As the person of the Trinity at work as God *within* the creature within creation, the Spirit is intensively present in the life of the believer, moving the believer within the movement of God.

This movement is not only a movement of being incorporated in Christ into the eternal loving of the Son by the Father and the Father by the Son (on the vertical axis); it is also (and perhaps mostly, from our perspective as creatures) the movement in which we move within the eternal gracious and unmerited loving of creation by God. In God's saving ways, there is a gracious and superabundant loving movement of God toward all that is not God in creation, reconciliation, and redemption. To be caught up in the way of God in the Spirit's work of salvation in creation is to be caught up in the way of God not only back to the eternal life of divine love but also, in the form of that divine love, outward on the horizontal plane of creation to love for creation. In this expression of love, the church is the first fruit of reconciliation and redemption in the church's creaturely conditions in the time before we share in the eternal life of God. In being brought by the Spirit's intensive indwelling into participation in the way of God's grace in the world, we come to move within the way of God's grace for the world. It is for this reason that the church is established as an event of the act of the Spirit. The church comes into being by being caught in the ways of grace and, by virtue of this and simultaneous to this, moves in the ways of grace in the world now. In this movement in which we move, we are moving to God but also at the same time to other people in the world in love, since that is the movement in which we are caught up.

The Community Form of the Movements of Grace

Dietrich Bonhoeffer's account of the social community describes this reality, though with less of an emphasis on the Holy Spirit than

I think might be helpful. For Bonhoeffer, relationships (or "sociality") stem from relationship with God. He writes: "Community with God by definition establishes social community as well. It is not that community with God subsequently leads to social community; rather, neither exists without the other. . . . The unbroken social community belongs to primal being . . . , in parallel to the eschatological hope we have for it in the church."[4] Although for Bonhoeffer these two moments of community with God and social community occur at once, their relationship needs nevertheless to be described in its asymmetry. It is God's own grace which enables humanity to share in communion with God and with others in the community. In a fallen world (suggested by Bonhoeffer's reference to "primal being"), this formation of community is not a properly natural propensity. Instead, it is a work of salvation; it belongs fully, not to the fallen creation, but to the redeeming, reconciling, and sanctifying grace of God in creation. Left to their own sinful devices, humans are possessed of the heart turned in on itself not only as it relates to God but also as it relates to other creatures. And even where societies exist, they do so often to diminish the possibility of competing hearts turned in on themselves (we might say to prevent war or anarchy); or else they exist for the good of the individuals who themselves benefit from the utility of cooperation (a corporate form of the heart turned in on itself); or they exist because of the attractiveness of other individuals, whom we like often because they are actually quite like us, or "our sorts of people" (an aggrandizement of the heart turned in on itself in light of the positive views of others who are like the self).

But the church should not be like that. I am always amazed, in fact often overwhelmed, by coffee after church. In one church I formerly attended, I remember coming into the hall after preaching and greeting the people following the service. I took just a moment to look around, and I was overcome almost to the point to tears. I looked at this one table where my grandmother sat. She (with her walking sticks) was helping a middle-aged man with Down syndrome to the table and was sorting out his tea and the particular two biscuits he always liked to have. Chatting with them at the table were a teenager and a man who was a judge. On the fringe of the same conversation was a retired woman with alcoholism (drunk as she always was), and a little farther down at the same table, but in another set of conversations, sat a lovely lady who had schizophrenia, another teenager, a mum of three, a retired headmaster, and a doctor. All kinds of people who would never have been put together or come together otherwise were all there in fellowship, drinking tea and coffee and chatting about life and their concerns. All of them were not only affirming each other's human dignity; they were also affirming each other as friends and fellow family members in God's own household. It was an image of what St. Paul is talking about in Galatians when we are told there is neither Jew nor Greek, male nor female, slave nor free, since now in our identity in Jesus Christ, in his body, we are all one (cf. Gal. 3:28). These sights are not uncommon in our churches (and where they are uncommon we should repent!), but they are remarkable glimpses of the human breadths of salvation. They are miracles of saving grace.

The Holy Spirit's saving work establishes genuine and reconciled human community in all its forms. It is an act of the breadth of the salvation of the God who creates the society of God. Community belongs to the gracious, redeeming work of God and not fallen creation. It is an anticipation proleptically, partially, and contingently of the redemption to come. Clearly, it is not only Christians who share in community. As rare as genuine community is, Christians have no monopoly on it, and the Bible itself testifies to the people of God in the community of Israel and the community of the church. After all, it is not the form of the community that is the precondition for the Spirit, but the Spirit who is the precondition for the community. The Spirit is Lord, and thereby free. But Christians do (by virtue of the Spirit who creates the church) share (by means of the salvific intensity of the Spirit's acting presence and indwelling in the creature who is being reconciled and redeemed) in genuine community in creation. This is a community which is given by God to be a community with God *and other humans* (indeed other creatures). This event of God is a reconciling and redeeming event this side of eternal life in anticipation of the kingdom that is to come. And we can actively participate in the benefits of this salvation now, sharing in the ministry of reconciliation with one another to which we are called (2 Cor. 5:18).

The Twofold Nature of the Greatest Commandments

The saving work of the Spirit orients us toward God and God's work of creation, reconciliation, and redemption and simultaneously and proportionately toward God's creation, which is reconciled in Christ and awaits its redemption. Jesus's teaching concerning the greatest commandment is this: "'You shall love the Lord your God with all your heart, and with all your soul, and with all your mind.' This is the greatest and first commandment. And a second is like it: 'You shall love your neighbor as yourself'" (Matt. 22:37–39). There is a vertical (God) and horizontal (neighbor) dimension to following the commandment of Christ—a commandment whose fulfillment reverses the reality of the fall and the individualized heart turned in toward itself. Following either part of this commandment is not something we can do unaided. But there is a further subtlety here. In Jesus's discourses in John, the disciples (in an analogy to the Johannine community) are given the commandment to love one another but in a very particular way: "I give you a new commandment, that you love one another. *Just as I have loved you,* you also should love one another. By this everyone will know that you are my disciples, if you have love for one another" (John 13:34–35, emphasis added). This love for the neighbor has a concrete and powerful form: it is the form of the love Christ has for his disciples. The form of this love is crucicentric: it takes the form of one who goes to the cross so as to lay down one's life for not only one's friends but even one's enemies. This discussion of love for one another in John comes before the beginning of the Farewell Discourses in which Jesus discusses the Paraclete (the Holy Spirit) who will come. This Paraclete will guide the disciples into all truth (John 16:13), including into the truth of love in its Christlike form. We come to share in this form by sharing in Christ's humanity through complete and total dependence on and being filled by the Spirit.

Salvation is not given as a commodity or an object or a teaching or a commandment from the heavenly life of God downward to the life of the creature. Salvation is, instead, that breadth of the eternal movement of the God of salvation as Father, Son, and Holy Spirit to act in the creation, reconciliation, and redemption of all that is not God. It is the constant and faithful movement time and time again toward and within creation in saving grace. And in this movement we are able to be moved by and to move with the Spirit, participating in this salvific movement and being brought by it into an active participation in the life, humanity, and body of Jesus Christ, the Son who is eternally loved by the Father. Through the event of the Spirit's intensive presence within us, we move in the ways of the Spirit and participate both in love of God and in love of those around us, whom God also loves.

The Church's Anticipation of Salvation in the Givenness of the Other

The church as a salvific event of the Spirit becomes a proleptic anticipation of this love for the other and orientation on God. The church is the first fruits of the inbreaking of God's future in the present. It is this in an intense and particular way—by virtue of the very *givenness* of the church's life and the community one finds within it. In its anticipatory form, the church has not yet arrived; the church in its fallenness and sin is always and ever anew being freed to participate in the redeeming and reconciling work of God.

But the church is that community in which the other is given as *a gift in her otherness* by the Spirit's saving grace. For our salvation, the Spirit creates the particular church in a particular time in its creaturely contingency and ordinariness. The Spirit does this so that we might express salvation not only in relation to God in worship and thanksgiving, and not only so that we might hear the gospel, but also so that we might love the other. This otherness is not an otherness like any in the world. This otherness is not based on what the other can do for us or on how much we might like them. Instead, this otherness is based on the very givenness of the other person in the very normal contexts in which we gather together to do the most intimate thing we can imagine—calling for the Holy Spirit to free us to participate in creation in the body of Christ and in Christ's self-giving for the other.

This very givenness of the other moves the individual beyond an understanding of salvation as simply the restoration of a broken vertical relationship with God toward an understanding of being caught up in salvation as the way of grace of the God of salvation, who turns the believer outward to both God (vertically) and creation (horizontally). The other in the church community whom we are freed to love as a genuine other is a precious gift of God's salvation (even in the other's weakness, fallenness, and propensity to sin, from which we can suffer). In this gift of the other, we work out our salvation in fear and trembling in the life of the Spirit, who creates the church as an event in which reconciliation and redemption are being brought about on the vertical plane of the creature's relationship with the Creator and on the horizontal plane of the creature's relationship to other creatures. That's why we share the peace at Holy Communion: we come *in communion* with one another to God, and we need to be at peace with our fellow brothers and sisters. In receiving God's love and loving God by participating in Christ in the eternal loving of the Father by the Son in the bond of union of the Spirit, and by participating in God's ways of gracious redeeming and reconciling, we who are being redeemed simultaneously receive the love of the given neighbor in the event of the church and give love to the given neighbor as well in interdependent ordinary lives.

The love that we receive as we are being redeemed is most profoundly the love of the fellowship of the church through and by another, simply because that other is given by God to be a fellow heir of God's kingdom. In this, God frees us as we are being redeemed from our hearts being turned in on themselves in the horizontal plane of our normal lives. In this, the givenness of the other becomes a place for the outworking of our own salvation, as the other can be to us the object of love simply because she is given by God. And in loving the other in her givenness, we can participate in the divine ways of loving grace through the Spirit's saving work.

This is all dependent on the saving act of the Spirit, through which it is brought about that the Spirit dwells intensively in us, freeing us for participation in God's loving ways both in relation to the trinitarian life (vertically) and in relation to the creaturely others in their givenness in the world (horizontally). It is not a natural occurrence but an event of salvation. Karl Barth, perhaps the greatest theologian since the Reformation, once wrote this:

> The members of the people of God should never imagine that they can and should help themselves and one another, exerting and forcing themselves to love one another. This kind of exertion is quite futile, since none can do it. Only by the Holy Spirit do they become free for this action. But by the Holy Spirit they do become free for it. By the Holy Spirit the individual becomes free for existence in an active relationship with the other in which he is loved and finds that he may love in return. The one who is most deeply filled with the Spirit is the one who is richest in love, and the one who is devoid of love necessarily betrays the fact that he is empty of the Spirit. Naturally, it is a matter of faith in the remission of sins, sins which

will be present even where men stand in this active connexion as Christians filled with the Spirit and with love.[5]

The reason this love of the given other is a work of saving grace through the act of the Spirit—and the place in which this most immediately comes into being is the church, in which we are presented with the other in her complete givenness as gift—is that in this we are being freed in anticipation of the total salvation and redemption we will one day receive. We are being freed in creation by saving grace from existing in sin not only in our broken (vertical) relationship with God but also in our broken (horizontal) relationship with the rest of creation. The event of the first fruits of the restoration of this horizontal rupture in sin is the church, as the Spirit acts in lives of believers to bring them to share in the body of Christ. This church is an event of the breadth of divine salvation in the breadth of creation and of our relations on the horizontal axis of creation.

Conclusion

Through the event of the Spirit's intensive indwelling in her life, the believer is restored to the lost humanity that she was always to have. She becomes a new creation to herself, but this is the creation God eternally determined her to be, as she is freed proleptically to participate in the eternal divine loving and grace in the present. This humanity which the Spirit's act brings about is not one in which there is enmity between individuals but is instead one in which all are one in the unity of the Spirit. There is peace as the Spirit allows the creature to move in the movements of grace and to share in the Father's and Son's love. As Ephesians 4 reminds us,

I therefore . . . beg you to lead a life worthy of the calling to which you have been called, with all humility and gentleness, with patience, bearing with one another in love, making every effort to maintain the unity of the Spirit in the bond of peace. There is one body and one Spirit, just as you were called to the one hope of your calling, one Lord, one faith, one baptism, one God and Father of all, who is above all and through all and in all. (Eph. 4:1–6)

The unity of the Spirit is the unity to which the believer is called. For that reason, the individual is not the first or even primary locus of saving grace; salvation is broader than that. To reconcile humanity and redeem humanity from the selfish desires of the heart turned in on itself determines that God gives us *community* as an event of the breadth of the Spirit's work of salvation. Humans are enabled to escape the effects of the fall in the world now through the Holy Spirit's redeeming grace. Indeed, the Spirit enables us to participate actively as humans in the divine life which as the great I AM has no self-preserving ego whatsoever. We come to share in the eternal life of the love of the Father and the Son in the bond of union of the Spirit, and the eternal life of the God who in creation, reconciliation, and redemption gives Godself to be for that which is not God.

In the Spirit's saving work in the concrete event of the church, horizontal relations begin to be reordered in the fundamental givenness of the other *as other* in the community of faith. In this the identity of the human being is saved from its life ordered toward itself. Individual alterity in relation to God and fellow humans is reversed by a salvific act of God, who makes us anew by God's grace in the life of the community of the church. This new life is that life to which the creature was eternally determined and from which we fell: new life is precisely a new life oriented toward the creatureliness it was supposed to have. This is why the church offers salvation—not because of itself and its forms but because it is the event which is the expression of the Spirit's act of turning our hearts out not only to God but simultaneously and proportionately to the given other. In our churches we must display this new reality of the gospel. There the prisoners must be set free, the downcast raised up, the brokenhearted cherished, the publican and the sinner and the prostitute treated as honored guests. Why? Because as believers share in the same Spirit, Christ is present in his body. And in Christ we are new creations in our relations with one another and our ministry of reconciliation.

3

The Breadth of Grace
for the World

In pointing in the previous chapter to our need to love the other in their created givenness, we already raised issues of the complexities of the breadth of the victory of Christ for the world. If the church is the body of Christ, sharing in the same Spirit who rested on Christ completely, what, then, does it mean for the church here and now to be that body which—when it was incarnate on earth—ate and drank with sinners and tax collectors, and proclaimed that prostitutes and tax collectors would enter the kingdom of God before the religious people of his own era? Are our imaginations of salvation too narrow, self-obsessed, and self-justifying for the nature of the gospel?

There is a wonderful story in *The Wisdom of the Desert Fathers*. A monk who lives as a hermit asks God if God is pleased with him. An angel appears and tells the monk that he isn't doing as well as the gardener in the city nearby. Given the extreme life of religious devotion the hermit had engaged in, he goes to the city, in some degree of confusion, to observe this ordinary gardener and work out what makes him special. Finding nothing special, the hermit asks the gardener if he can go to his house for dinner. At dinner he pushes and pushes the gardener to tell him about his life and what makes him special. In the end, a little cross, the gardener tells the monk about his life, but still the hermit cannot see anything special. The story concludes as follows:

> As they were eating in the evening, the old man [hermit] heard people in the road singing songs because the gardener's house was in a busy spot. So the old man said to him, "Brother, you want to live for God, so how do you stay in this place and how can you not be disturbed when you hear them singing these songs?" The gardener said, "I confess to you, Father, I have never been troubled or shocked." At these words, the old man said, "What, then, do you think to yourself when you hear these things?" The other replied, "I think that all will go into the Kingdom." When he heard this, the elder was amazed and said, "This is the act which outstrips my many years of labour."[1]

We should dare to hope that salvation is wider and broader and higher and deeper than we ever might imagine.

Now, let me be clear here. I am not in any way advocating some unnuanced, dogmatic form of universalism—the idea that faith and life are insignificant and that everyone receives salvation and its effects come what may and regardless of anything. My concern is rather that we do not fall into the trap of thinking that the judgment which belongs to God alone belongs to us or can be made by us. We need to understand the primacy of God's action of grace and the asymmetry of human action in relation to that grace, including even that of placing faith in that grace. The church and the faithful are not the *causes* of grace but rather—for all their significance—the *recipients* of grace who move within grace's movements. We can never forget that we are the beneficiaries of the breadth of this salvation, not the conditions for it. My concern, one might say, is not dogmatic overconfidence in divine grace which captures saving grace in a rule greater than itself (that is, that all people are unquestionably saved), but a more humble and cautious sense that if salvation can even reach me, we might dare to hope for all. This stems from a profound sense of the mystery and inexhaustibility of the intense and ungraspable glory and majesty of God, who is our salvation.

One way to think about this is through the idea of the asymmetry of gravitational forces. I am told (though I am certainly no physicist!) that when an object like a ball is dropped, it is the magnitude of the earth's gravitational pull which draws that ball down to the earth. But at the very last moment, the ball itself (small as it is in relation to the vastness of the whole earth) asserts a very small pull—a tiny, almost immeasurable force—upon the magnitude of the force of gravity and then becomes part of that gravitational pull of the earth. God's immense and overwhelming gracious movement toward creation and our human response to it are perhaps best thought of in terms similar to the asymmetry of these physical forces. When we consider ourselves—even in our faith—the center of our own universe, we fall straight back into the fallenness of the heart turned in on itself. Our call within the church is to share with the world the good news of Jesus Christ, the Son of God, Pantocrator (ruler of all), reconciler and savior of the world, who desires that *tiny* movement from creation. We are not called to make everything about the tiny movement: we preach Jesus Christ and him crucified. We are to see our own faith and response to God with a profound sense of that disproportionality.

The Keys of the Kingdom

The Priority of God's Grace, Not Human Action

Indeed, the concern about judgments that belong to God alone being relocated to the church visible is at the heart of the Reformation and the founding of the Protestant churches. While the Reformation is often recounted to us in terms of the primacy of Scripture or of justification by grace through faith, or by accounts of the Reformers' interpretations of the sacraments, it is certainly also the case (and perhaps even more foundationally the case) that the Reformation was in response to a perceived overconfidence of the pre-Reformation church's capacity to see and interpret itself as the kingdom of God. The Reformation entailed a profound criticism of the propensity within the church to understand the human actions of the church as conditioning the reception of divine saving grace. There is a repeated refrain in the writings of Martin Luther to this end concerning the keys of the kingdom. The pre-Reformation church had interpreted Jesus's injunction to Peter in Matthew 16:19—in which he is told he has the keys of the kingdom such that whatever he binds or looses on earth will be bound or loosed in heaven—as a statement about the church's nature and authority through the successors of Peter in the popes of Rome and those who derive authority from the pope. Luther fiercely rejected the idea of the church holding the power of the keys, recognizing instead the primacy of God and God's grace and judgment, which are invisible before they are visible and not conditioned on human actions or the church's actions.

These concerns primarily have to do with the relationship between divine and human action in the church—and particularly, that these not be conflated. The church is not imbued with the rights and powers of the divine, such that it feels able to make judgments about salvation which belong to God alone. All human action, for the Reformers, remains continually and constantly dependent on God and God's grace as its basis. They considered it necessary to firmly guard the difference and distinguish between God's action and human action. For them, one absolutely could not conflate the church with the kingdom, and the church did not have the right to do so. It could not offer indulgences to buy people out of purgatory, or offer absolutions given by a priest that were binding on God. But equally, the church could also not conflate its own expanse with the expanse of the kingdom. In the first place, the church is invisible before it is visible—hidden before it is revealed. It is known only in faith. The reason for this has to do with where grace resides and the asymmetric relationship between divine action and human action. Grace resides with God, who freely lavishes it on creation. Grace cannot be grace—it cannot be absolutely free loving-kindness—if it is something we condition or cajole God into.

Analogies of Grace

I often tell churches that grace is like one of three scenarios if you get caught speeding in your car. The first scenario is that you are doing 80 mph in a 70 mph zone. You are doing 80 mph because you (wrongly) believe that the police won't stop you for that because your speedometer could be off by 10 mph or so. Nevertheless, the blue lights come on behind you. You get pulled over. You are issued a ticket. You are polite to the police officer. You pay the fine. You take the points on your license. And the cost is settled. That is a scenario of justice: you do wrong; you get caught; you suffer the consequences.

The second scenario is that you doing 80 mph in a 70 mph zone for the same reason—you think you can get away with it. Once again the blue lights flash, and you are pulled over. But you are quick-thinking. You roll down your window, and just before the police officer is about to issue the fine, you stop him. "I'm terribly sorry, officer, but I don't normally speed. It's just that my wife is about to have a baby, and I'm desperately trying to get to the hospital." The officer tells you in response that you shouldn't be speeding, but he can understand that this is a stressful situation. He lets you off, given the circumstances. That is a scenario of mercy. (The only problem is, you've not been truthful, and—when the police officer offers to accompany you to the hospital so you aren't held up by traffic—you have to go into the maternity ward and pretend someone who is not your wife is your wife!)

The third scenario runs something like this. You are doing 100 mph in a 70 mph zone after a terrible day at work. You see the blue lights flash behind you, and for just a moment you wonder if you could put your foot down and get away. But realizing you are driving an old one-liter engine, you think the better of it. So, you pull over. The officer comes to your window, but before he has even opened his notebook, you start shouting: "This is the problem with the country! Police are more interested in fining good drivers like me than they are in catching rapists and murderers. You should be ashamed of yourself doing this job when there is probably some poor old granny out there being robbed! Instead, you are punishing a good law-abiding citizen like myself. Anyway, it's people who drive too slowly that you should be concerned about, not good drivers like me. You know, if this were a sensible country like Germany, there wouldn't even be speed limits on major roads . . ." On and on you rail at this officer until you finally run out of steam. The officer gently puts his hands up and softly tells you that you have done wrong. You try to have another go at him. But with a quiet and firm dignity, he continues. He says that you have done wrong and that you are going to have a big fine and a lot of penalty points on your license. But if you just come with him now, he says to your amazement, he personally will pay the fine and take the points onto his license for you. And when you get to the police station, he makes you a coffee and gives you a box of chocolates, polishes your shoes, and lets you off scot-free. Grace is something like that—absolutely unmerited, absolutely free loving-kindness.

The Response to Grace as a Response, Not a Cause

Nothing conditions God to act in grace. It is how God is and who God is. It is God's way with creation. The gracious act of God *makes possible* the act of the human *by response*, but the human act does not contain or make possible the grace of God. God's saving action is the condition for human activity; human activity is not the condition for God's saving activity of grace. The danger for evangelical faith is that we make a work of our faith. When we do that, we replicate the error of the pre-Reformation church in believing ourselves already to be synonymous with the kingdom, and therefore able to tell where the Spirit's presence frees us to participate in the benefits of Christ's salvation. We have failed to free ourselves from a doctrine of the keys, however distinctly we express this in evangelical cultures compared to medieval Roman Catholic ones. We identify this grace all too often as uniquely in our own churches, in those who believe what we believe (especially the particular model of the atonement!), in those who pray the believers' prayer in the same way we do, in those who have received baptism. Important as all these things are, they are not the limits of or conditions for the saving work of God. The only limits and conditions are found in the immeasurable height and breadth and depth of God's grace for the creation.

For evangelicals (my own people), the same is true of conversion. Now, I can tell you the exact moment when I knew absolutely the grace of God in my life. I was eight years old, and it is the clearest thing I remember of my childhood. But the centrality of grace determines that conversion should never be understood as a work. Conversion is, instead, a *response* to God's graciousness which recognizes that grace as freely given, unmerited, and undeserved—that is, as gracious. The prevenience of grace to conversion reminds us of this: grace is already present before we are converts, and it is to that grace that we respond. The initiator of our conversion is not the self but the God who makes Godself known by the power of God's Holy Spirit, the God who always turns toward us and desires us to turn to Godself. A convert's response to God is only ever a response which is at best abductive—that is, a response which involves moving toward or turning toward the God who in God's movement of grace to us attracts us to move (just that tiny amount God calls us to) toward Godself. Conversion is not a work which conditions God into salvation but a response to God to whom salvation properly belongs: "Salvation belongs to our God who is seated on the throne, and to the Lamb!" (Rev. 7:10). Salvation does not belong to our conversion; salvation belongs to the saving God.

An Appropriate Confidence and Humility in the Church's Response

This principle applies also to the church's understanding of the breadth of salvation with regard to the church. No institution or form or organization can be said to be *fully* representative of the action of God or to be the basis on which the true presence of God can be absolutely assured. In calling to mind the event of the church as an act of the Spirit, order is important. The Spirit is the *condition* for the church's coming into being. But it is not that the act of the Spirit is present only in the event of the church or limited to it. There is more to the dynamic, self-determining act of the Holy Spirit than the church, and the church cannot simply be identified with the Spirit or salvation. We must faithfully attend to God's activity, but we must guard against overconfidence that human activity is the condition of or even *is* divine activity. The church's creaturely forms cannot be the basis for, nor straightforwardly identified with, the Spirit's presence or the salvific grace of Christ. Rather, despite the human propensity to sin and idolatry, it comes to pass that, in the Spirit's gracious faithfulness, the Spirit acts faithfully to bring about the event of the life of the believer as she shares in the benefits of Christ's reconciliation.

The church and the life of the believer are events which take place in creaturely space and time in the condition of creaturely fallenness as it is being reconciled and redeemed. That it is an *event* of the act of the Spirit in the human conditions in which the church comes into being should help prevent us from believing the church to be possessed of direct authority from or of God, or possessed of the rights of identifying (with its keys) who is or is not in the kingdom. The church is not the kingdom of God, nor is the church a perfect society. The church is that community which God chooses, out of God's grace and for God's gracious purposes, to create as a witness to the world of God's saving desire for the creation.

We must nevertheless remember simultaneously that the church and the life of the believer are brought into being by the Spirit. The cause of the believer's and the church's becoming is an act of the Holy Spirit. It is crucial to remember that it is not the church or the believer which causes the Spirit to come. There is also a danger from the Protestant (and particularly evangelical) context of certain behaviors being considered essential to bringing about the presence of the Holy Spirit, rather than being preceded and thereby caused by the Spirit. Such conditions vary in time and place and from denomination to denomination. It may be a particular mode of worship that unwittingly but constantly presents the "conditions" for the descent of the Spirit in a charismatic context; or it may be the purity of life of the faithful who are gathered which is considered the precondition for the Spirit's coming, as in Puritan groups; or it may be assent to a particular set of doctrines or, as discussed in the first chapter of this book, subscribing to a particular model of salvation; and so forth. But nothing conditions God's Spirit for God's gracious and salvific act. The Lord is free and gracious, and as the church, as believers, we are called simply to *respond* to the Spirit and to call on the Spirit to help us learn what it means to say, "Jesus is Lord." It is God who fits us for God's salvation and who fits us to meet together and to come into being despite our and our community's sinfulness, the poverty of our worship, and our unacknowledged propensities to idolatry. In its faith, the church is called to be the place which, in calling for the coming of the Spirit, offers itself as Mary did upon news of the descent of the Holy Spirit for the conception of Jesus (Luke 1:35) with the words "Here am I,

the servant of the Lord" (1:38). It is the *act of the Spirit* which is the
cause of the event of the church.

The Primacy of the Living God

Certainly, many Christians after the Reformation have been nerv-
ous of speaking about and conflating divine and human action in
the church and in the life of the believer. This is an important insight. God's work is greater than we can ever imagine. But the danger
simultaneously has been that such accounts have also proceeded
without a fulsome account of God's agency, the Spirit's work. In
characteristically forceful manner, Christoph Friedrich Blumhardt
lambasts the church's negligence of the dynamic liveliness of the
divine life. While he accepts that there has been much talk of the
church and its teachings, of denominations and their forms, he gives
a clarion call for us to move from speech about our religious self-
fulfillment and perpetuation (as "the ones that look out for their
own salvation") to speech about the livingness of God:

> God is dead, murdered. Nietzsche experienced more truth in his
> wrought-up nerves than all the boring Christians, who don't have a
> serious thought left for God! God is of no real importance, even for
> people with religion, because religion has become more important
> than God. Though people get into tremendous arguments about re-
> ligious questions, all the time God is dead. And it is perfectly all right
> with them if he is dead, because then they can do what they like. . . .
>
> But that is just it: God in Christ is not dead; he still is the Alpha
> and the Omega.[2]

Here, order is once again and as always absolutely key. To speak of
the faith and the church as events of the act of the Spirit is to give the
Spirit lordship over the church and the believer and all speech about
the church and the believer. There can be no pure identification of
God, God's kingdom, and God's salvation with the institution of the

church and those who visibly profess the faith. There are, as Luther reminds us, many sheep without and wolves within. But God still does something powerful through God's own gloriously alive life in the believer and in the church.

Put formally, while the Spirit is the sine qua non of the church and the believer, the church and the believer are not the sine qua non of the Spirit. This aphorism seeks to capture not only the non-limitation of the Spirit to the church but also the appropriate foundational and relational order between the Spirit and the church. It is an aphorism that does us well with regard also to the breadth of salvation and the surprises of the grace of the victory of Jesus.

The Complexity of New Testament Judgment Imagery

The Life of Jesus as a Challenge to Our Presumptions

Indeed, this aphorism captures not only something of the Scripture's teaching that the Spirit blows where the Spirit wills, but also something of the benefits of Christ's reconciliation and salvation in eternal life, known to us now by the event of the Spirit's activity. This does not mean that we should try to speak in some binding, dogmatic way about the extent of God's salvation. Instead, we should speak of the breadth of salvation in the *personhood* of God, who (rather than the church or any action of the believer) is the total and complete Savior. In speaking of salvation, we should speak of God's freedom, of God's sovereignty, of God's lordship, of God as Judge, and not of our own proclivities to make judgments which belong to God alone.

The narrative of Scripture testifies to God's personhood and God's activity with God's people. Thus, rather than establishing principles that flow from the abstracted theological idea of God's grace and salvation, we do better (as chap. 1 argues) to attend to the *person* of Jesus Christ to seek hints for our theological speech and our ethical

and ecclesial behavior in the narrative of his life, death, and resurrection. In the particularity of Jesus's person and teaching, we may
well perceive something of the complexity of the tension pointed
to already regarding not treating the visible form of the church or
the visible expression of faith as the delimiting factor of salvation's
breadth and of God's free grace. Jesus's attitude to those who might
be perceived to be outsiders to the kingdom of God (sinners, prostitutes, tax collectors, Samaritans, and gentiles) presents a situation
which is far from easy for us in the contemporary church to summa-
rize in our usual terms. Christ's relationships with those who seem to
be outsiders to the kingdom are person-to-person encounters over
which no one but Christ, together with his Father and his Spirit, has
an overview. We make judgments like the Pharisees in Scripture all
the time—just over different issues. We make judgments about who
are the insiders to salvation, usually presuming that they are like us.
So we need to ask ourselves the following question with all the urgency of the gospel: Who are the sinners, prostitutes, tax collectors,
Samaritans, and gentiles of our own contexts and age—those we
judge but whom Christ knows and intimately loves?

Insiders and Outsiders Today

The contexts of Jesus, who spoke to the religious people and
institutions of his own age, need to be reappropriated and rein-
terpreted today. We do well to consider who it is that Jesus speaks
against in our own times. If God's Word continues to speak to us,
surely we cannot simply take the words of Jesus that are directed
at the institutional insiders of his own day (the priests, the Pharisees, the Sadducees, for example) as historical statements about one
particular and singular instance of religiosity in his own cultural
context. If God continues to speak to us by the power of the Holy
Spirit through God's Word, we must ask the question when faced
with Jesus's assertions about judgment: Where are *we* in this text as
God addresses us? What is perhaps most uncomfortable is that as

self-confessed religious, or the faithful, or the religious insiders of our own generation (as Christians), we may be like those in Scripture who presume that they are the furthest inside but in reality may not be. Might we be the Pharisees of today? Do we run the danger of assuming we are always the insiders while we simultaneously exclude others and play God in thinking we are able to make eschatological judgments about them?

The Gospel's Challenge to Our Judgments

Throughout the Gospels, we are able to see this danger and complexification in those who perceive themselves as insiders finding their self-perceived confidence in their position before God. Jesus is not only treated as an outsider, but he also proclaims the kingdom of God to be for those we might perceive as outsiders. It is the prostitutes and tax collectors, the perceived outsiders (and it's worth remembering that the text does not say, "Those who used to be . . ."), who will enter the kingdom of God *before* (not, notably, *instead of*) those who are perceived to be, and perceive themselves to be, the insiders (Matt. 21:31). There is a broadening here for our imaginations of the breadth of salvation in Christ. And we must be wary of simply ignoring the judgments pronounced on the scribes and Pharisees as if they were directed only to these historical groups. The living nature of Scripture means that these judgments must be understood afresh for those of us who might also be judged under the harsh words of Jesus: "Woe to you. . . . For you lock people out of the kingdom of heaven. For you do not go in yourselves, and when others are going in, you stop them. . . . For you cross sea and land to make a single convert, and you make the new convert twice as much a child of hell as yourselves" (Matt. 23:13, 15). It seems that for the religious of Jesus's time and for ourselves, this saying is sure: judgment begins in the house of God (cf. 1 Pet. 4:17).

Lest, indeed, we think that these charges apply only to historical figures in New Testament times and that to see them as otherwise is to engage in flights of interpretative fancy, Jesus presents us with a discussion about these issues which points not only backward in history but also forward to the apocalypse. In some of Jesus's most disturbing binary language, we can see at a future point (and not simply a past one) a level of surprise by those who presume themselves to be insiders. As those who live before the final judgment, these warnings surely apply equally as strongly to us as to Jesus's contemporaries. In short, in Jesus's pointing to the future judgment, we as the church are even historically here in the text.

In some of the seemingly clearest indicators of Jesus's binary approaches to eschatology, we read about both the sheep and the goats saying, "Lord, when was it that we saw you hungry or thirsty or a stranger or naked or sick or in prison, and did not take care of you?" (Matt. 25:44; cf. 25:37–39). Evidently, the final determination of the individual is not simply based on any empirical visibility as to which section of humanity we belong to prior to the judgment (whether that be through the church or through some dogmatic assent or profession of conversion). Instead, it is based on the way in which we treat the least of Jesus's brothers and sisters. This appears to lead to surprise and questioning of Jesus's judgment: those who expect to be sheep find themselves as goats, and those who expect to be goats find themselves as sheep. Clearly, there is no easy equating of those who in history are seen to be on the inside or outside with those who at the end find themselves on the inside or outside, respectively. Matters are a little more complex than that.

The danger in pointing to such verses for our tradition is that all too easily we can slip into a movement away from grace back again toward a works-based approach to salvation. However, evangelical "activism" (the behavior toward others in good works which should arise *from* the assurance of salvation) is an activism which flows *from faith and is enabled by faith*, and which is possible through the Spirit's prevenient gracious work. Indeed, the context of Jesus's words here might seem to point in that direction: the sheep inherit the kingdom which was prepared for them from the foundation of the world (Matt. 25:34), and thus at a deeper level not one which simply becomes theirs by virtue of their actions. How best to understand these acts is not a straightforward issue; this is no simple works-based understanding of salvation. But it is equally not an account of salvation which confuses the correct *belief about* justification by faith alone with *the grace that justifies* through faith. It shows us that judgment belongs to God *alone*, and while assurance has a significant place in assuring us of our salvation through the Spirit's presence, it should not assure us of the condemnation of others whom we might well discover God knows and sees as sheep even when we adjudge them goats. My concern is neither devaluing conversion, the church, assurance, and faith, nor dogmatically proclaiming all to be saved. My concern is to acknowledge that God, who is free and sovereign, is judge in these things.

The Surprises of Grace

When I was a student, I was told a story by a Protestant minister in the city. A young man had been a heroin addict and a criminal. He would steal and rob (at times violently) in order to get the drugs and had been in prison for his crimes. Then he started coming to church and heard the gospel, coming to faith in Christ. All was going well, but he fell back into his drug addiction and into the criminal behaviors which fed it. Unable to cope with this alongside what he had learned of his new life in Christ, the man—overcome with guilt—committed suicide.

When the day of the funeral came, my friend the minister was due to conduct the service and was waiting outside the church for the coffin. He was dreading having to speak and was unsure what it was he could possibly say in such a terrible circumstance. A road sweeper, dirty and unclean, walked past and asked the minister, who must have looked overwhelmed, if he was OK. The minister said, "No. This terrible, terrible thing has happened." He explained the circumstance and then said, "And I do not know what to say or how I can get through conducting this funeral." The road sweeper clapped his filthy hand on the arm of the minister's cassock and prayed: "Jesus, Mary, and Joseph, help this here father to do what you have told him he needs to. Give him strength to get this through this funeral." Following his unorthodox prayer, the man walked off.

The minister conducted the funeral in no small part enlivened and strengthened by the simple but strange prayer of the road sweeper. At the end of the act of cremation, the minister went into the vestry in the crematorium and there burst into a flood of tears—so much so that the carpet was wet as the salt water flowed from his eyes. As he sobbed, another minister walked into the vestry following another funeral. "Oh," said the other minister, "I hadn't realized anyone was here. I'll leave you be," and out he walked, leaving my friend in his great distress.

I wonder how God, who sees who the sheep and the goats are, sees that most complex of complex stories which we find so easy to judge. For those looking from the outside, it might seem easy to identify the religious insiders and the undesirables (including potentially the man in the coffin). But the role of the church is so much more complex in this story. Our judgment should only be one which involves a holy silence that trusts in the wisdom of God, who sees and knows the hearts of humans.

At Once Justified and Sinners

The Breadth of Sinfulness

This raises as well the issue of how we deal with the continued sin in believers in relation to the breadth of salvation. In our state as those reconciled by grace through faith, we remain, in the words of Martin Luther, *simul iustus et peccator* (at once justified and sinful).

But the continued sin we have in our *simul* state is such that we are not only culpable for our own sin but—by bringing sin into the world—also culpable for the propagation of the sin of others. The grace which saves and justifies us covers not only the sins we engage in but also the sin which we bring into the world. It is not simply as a result of the heinousness of the first and original sin that presently humanity sins. As human beings, as part of the human race within creation, all humanity falls with each sin; none of us is different from Adam or Eve. There is no exoneration of our individual sin by virtue of the common experience of sinfulness. We can't simply blame a fall in ancient times for our current sinfulness. Our sin is bound up in that fall as much as the fall is bound up in our sin. In sinning, we too originate and propagate and cause sin as much as we are affected by it. Our sin is interconnected inextricably with all sin in the world. This is not only because we are all affected by original sin but because, in our sinning, we affect humanity in the untold and almost ungraspable effects our own sin has in creating sin. When we confess our sin and seek to receive the benefits of salvation, we need to do so with a sense of the breadth of our sinfulness and the breadth of God's saving grace.

I try to explain this to my students in the following way. I am a great fan of the Scandinavian crime drama *The Killing*. It is excellent TV (the best thing I've seen for a long time). It also offers a profoundly deep insight into the chaotic and self-perpetuating nature of sin. The premise of *The Killing* is the investigation of a murder that has already happened. It begins with the story of the murder and a series of other seemingly disconnected stories. What one comes to see is the cancerous nature of evil and how one murder has the capacity to create evil and sin not only in relation to the action of the murderer but in relation to all kinds of people two, three, four, five degrees of separation along the line. These are not only those affected by the sins of others but also those who—in response to those sins—themselves sin and self-perpetuate sin, which spreads ever more broadly and has further effects at all kinds of degrees of separation. The series ends (spoiler alert) with another murder caused (though in surprising ways) by the murder with which the story began. There is a very profound sense of the inescapability and self-perpetuating nexus of sin, and also of the reality that we cannot know the sinful effects of our own sinning in relation to the suffering of others, or the capacity of our own sin to lead to the sinning of others. This is the reality of living in a world tainted by original sin: Pandora's box has been opened.

The Breadth of Confession and Forgiveness

In this context, there is much worth to the prayer of confession of John Wesley:

> Forgive them all, O Lord:
> our sins of omission and our sins of commission;
> the sins of our youth and the sins of our riper years;
> the sins of our souls and the sins of our bodies;
> our secret and our more open sins;
> our sins of ignorance and surprise,
> and our more deliberate and presumptuous sins;
> the sins we have done to please ourselves
> and the sins we have done to please others;
> the sins we know and remember,
> and the sins we have forgotten;
> the sins we have striven to hide from others
> and the sins by which we have made others offend;
> forgive them, O Lord, forgive them all for his sake,
> who died for our sins and rose for our justification,
> and now stands at thy right hand to make intercession for us,
> Jesus Christ our Lord. Amen.[3]

But even this, far be it from me to suggest as a Methodist, does not go far enough. We confess not only our own sin but also our bringing sin into the world in its capacity to self-perpetuate and cause others to sin. I think evangelicalism needs to recover the breadth of this. So often we are so focused on the individual and individual culpability and responsibility that we forget the breadth of our capacity to bring sin into the world and to self-perpetuate it.

I am struck by our capacity to do this in relation to financial ethics. Despite the immense frequency with which the New Testament addresses issues of finance and debt and generosity, we repeatedly fail in the church and as believers to address the social component of our sinfulness in our contribution to systems of usury and unethical use of finances. Despite what the New Testament says about storing up treasures in heaven, we have spiritualized the teaching of Christ and spoken of stewardship and have failed to confess either that we contribute to an unjust system or that we cause the sins of others through that injustice. I am struck by this every time I receive a pension update, when I am asked about investing my pension pot and only one of the seven or eight options lists itself as "ethical." I am also aware of this whenever I renew my mortgage, with the difficulty of finding an "ethical" provider. Simply in engaging in both of these systems, there is a buying into a system based on investment, usury, and lack of faith. We so easily, almost unavoidably, are part of the form of structural sin which affects us, but to which we also contribute and which, in all kinds of ways we cannot imagine, leads to the self-perpetuation of sin in the world and the lives of others. There is a need for us to confess our sins and our causing of others to sin with a sense of the breadth of God's salvation. Salvation deals with the nexus and interconnection of human sinfulness, and we are justified for our sins *and* our contribution to the sins of others.

But What about Faith and Salvation?

We may say that that is all well and good, but the issue is not the interrelation of sin; the issue is the forgiveness of those sins through faith. I wonder, however, whether this sufficiently accounts for the interconnection of sin and unbelief. Because, ultimately, there is surely a sense that sin is unbelief—is faithlessness. We sin because we are faithless, because we place our trust elsewhere than in the saving grace of God, because we do not have our hope in the God of our salvation. Unbelief is not simply some form of questioning knowledge or uncertain intellectual assent (whatever that might mean); unbelief *is* faithlessness, is sin, is our capacity not to live in the reality of the grace of the gospel.

There can be no crude distinction between faith and works in this way. Christians cannot simply understand their continued sin as being canceled out by their faith; rather, their continued sin is indicative of their continued faithlessness and unbelief, which they share with a fallen and unbelieving and unfaithful world. For the question of salvation and the imputation of the righteousness of God, there can be no easy recourse to the *sola fide* (only by faith) in such a way that it separates faithlessness from sinfulness. We sin because we are faithless; we are faithless because we sin.

The recognition of the faithlessness even of the Christian determines that there can be no straightforward distinction in salvation from sin between the believing who continue in sin (as those who assent to the Christian faith) and the unbelieving who sin. Our continued faithlessness, our continued unbelief as those who are *simul iustus et peccator* (at once justified and sinful), *is our sinfulness.* Even in speaking of our salvation, we need to be aware constantly of our unbelief as Christians, even personally. This is perhaps most famously summarized in Karl Barth's comments on the atheism of Max Bense: "I know the rather sinister figure of the 'atheist' very well, not only from books, but also because it lurks somewhere inside me too."[4] We must remember that we are children of God by grace through Jesus Christ and faith in him. But we are these children constantly as we depend on the breadth of God's grace. This opens us not only to our difference from the rest of the world but also to our unity with the world in shared unbelief and faithlessness, because almost every moment of every day we are being constantly and continually rescued anew from the unbelief we share with the whole world. Christian faith is the enactment of the cry, "I believe; help my unbelief" (Mark 9:24). No false or crude categorization of the believing and the unbelieving can be made.

A Wise Humility

As we have learned from our discussion of the sheep and the goats in Matthew 25, perhaps the real precariousness in gaining God's salvation lies with those who are thought to be comfortably in a situation of faith. With an apocalyptic tone, Barth asserts,

> Christians who regard themselves as big and strong and rich and even dear and good children of God, Christians who refuse to sit with their Master at the table of publicans and sinners, are *not* Christians at all, have still to become so, and need not be surprised if heaven is gray above them and their calling upon God sounds hollow and finds no hearing.[5]

This seems appropriate given the New Testament's warnings to the scribes and Pharisees, with whom we might associate many contemporary Christians. As in the story of the rich man and Lazarus in Luke 16, Christians, too, may find themselves in the fearful position of the rich man's five brothers. Christians know and have had the warnings of Scripture, and if they have not heeded them, what hope may be expected? Those brothers were also, after all, people of faith in some sense—children of Abraham who had the words of Moses and the prophets. And so Barth continues:

> Only the eyes of the blind can be opened, only the ears of the deaf can be unstopped, only the lame can be told to take up their bed

and walk. . . . Only for prisoners is there liberation . . . , only for the hungry and thirsty is there the promise of being filled. . . . Only to those who take a low place can the call come: "Friend, go up higher." . . . To Christians who will not call upon God as those who are blind, deaf, lame, prisoners, hungry, and thirsty, *and who will not take the lowest place*, those acts of salvation cannot apply and will not happen.[6]

This same sentiment is also found in a powerful way in the Reformer and great advocate of justification by grace through faith, Martin Luther. Let me quote him:

> God receives none but those who are forsaken, restores health to none but those who are sick, gives sight to none but the blind, and life to none but the dead. He does not give saintliness to any but sinners, nor wisdom to any but fools. In short: He has mercy on none but the wretched and gives grace to none but those who are in disgrace. Therefore no arrogant saint, or just or wise man can be material for God, neither can he do the work of God, but he remains confined within his own work and makes of himself a fictitious, ostensible, false, and deceitful saint, that is, a hypocrite.[7]

The point is not simply that God's love can touch even the most unlovely (true as that may be), but rather more acutely that the Christian is likely to be that most unlovely of persons—the one who knows the good she should do but fails to do it (cf. Rom. 7). The role of the Christian is to acknowledge this and to say, "Woe is me; Father, forgive me for all the sin I have committed and all the sinning I have caused." Salvation will come only to the Christian who does "take the lowest place," falling on her knees and asking for the unmerited grace of God. The hope of salvation is not grounded in our works or actions or even our sense of religious superiority but is grounded instead in Christ who as Pantocrator is victorious.

The Place of the Assurance of Faith in a Fallen World

What, then, does it mean for the Christian in her faithlessness, and in not only her shared sin in the world but her causing sin in the world, to be assured of her salvation? Does all assurance determine a superiority which radically de-assures us of our reliance on the saving grace which comes only from Christ? Certainly, assurance is not about a self-confident approach to God and the gifts of God, nor is it a single momentary confirmation of our salvation to carry us through life. Instead, the first mark of assurance is the conviction of sin in the lives of believers. The prevenience of grace offers us assurance in the capacity to fall on our knees, not in superiority but in humility, to pray: "Father, forgive me through your Son's death. May I know the unmerited benefits of your grace through the presence of your Holy Spirit."

John Wesley, who placed such emphasis on assurance in his theology and spirituality, describes the assured believer in the following terms:

> The Scriptures describe that joy in the Lord which accompanies the witness of his Spirit as an humble joy, a joy that abases to the dust; that makes a pardoned sinner cry out, "I am vile! . . ." And wherever lowliness is, there is meekness, patience, gentleness, long-suffering. There is a soft, yielding spirit, a mildness and sweetness, a tenderness of soul which words cannot express. But do these fruits attend that *supposed* testimony of the Spirit in a presumptuous man? Just the reverse.[8]

When we do not, in being conscious of God's presence in our spirit, repent, but become confident of our assurance and grow haughty in our behavior, Wesley proclaims to us: "Discover thyself, thou poor self-deceiver! Thou who art confident of being a child of God. . . . O cry unto him, that the scales may fall off thine eyes."[9] Assurance comes not *after* the act of repentance but *in the very act of repentance*. Only in hearing the sentence of death do Christians hear the living, saving, and gracious voice of the one who says, "Your sins are forgiven."

And this relationship of repentance and assurance is far from a single moment or event; it is, rather, a continuous state of being in the life of the Christian, who every night should fall on her knees in confession to the Holy God and every morning do much the same. In St. Paul's language, the Spirit is a "guarantee" or "deposit" (*arrabōn*) of a future reality of salvation (2 Cor. 1:22; 5:5), and what we are given now is just that—a deposit and a guarantee, not the totality of the thing itself. In the present, we believe in salvation to eternal life in the midst of the valley of death. But it lies ahead of us now. What we are given for the present is the guarantee of it, the assurance of it—the assurance of hope. Since we possess it as a hope, we can never become arrogant or treat it as a right or something we deserve. We have it always in anticipation, always in the present which awaits its future. And we should guard it as the greatest treasure, thank God for it every day, and confess our faithlessness in our continued sin—even in knowing its power and reality—each morning and each night. Assurance of salvation for the Christian is a state of continually crying out to God in repentance, as opposed to a state of confidence in one's status on the basis of some singular event.

In contrast to understandings of assurance focused on our self-assured interiority as we concentrate on our personal, individualized salvation, assurance resting in God's grace and in the sufficiency of Christ has the capacity to be radically focused away from the self and toward others (as we discussed at length in chap. 2). We receive assurance precisely so that we are freed from being self-occupied and self-centered in our understandings of salvation. Martin Luther tells us, indeed, that those who lack assurance are in fact those who are self-centered. When we know the assurance of salvation, we are freed from concerning ourselves with our own self-preservation and can live lives focused on the good of others. John Wesley similarly argues that being assured of salvation expresses itself in loving our neighbors, in being kind to all humanity, and in living a life of gentleness and forbearance.

This means, further, that assurance is given as a gift for the loving of humanity; therefore, ironically perhaps, the activity of loving our neighbors and *all* humankind is a basis by which one might know that one is assured. If as Christians we are freed to love those around us, we are freed from the fear of wrath and the preoccupation with the salvation of ourselves. John Wesley presses this point. To know assurance we must be "embracing every child of man with earnest, tender affection, so as to be ready to lay down our life for our brother, as Christ laid down his life for us."[10] It is this activity (along with the activity of loving God) which gives believers a sense of the reality of their lives being conformed by the Spirit into the likeness of Jesus Christ.

This pattern of thought structurally seems to follow 1 John 4: because God has loved us, we are able to love God; and because of God's love toward us, we ought to love one another. Therefore, we know God in loving other people, and if we fail to love other people, we fail to know and love God. In our concrete existence as believers, we may know that we are assured if we genuinely love our neighbor, because only God's love is capable of allowing us truly to do so. If we love our neighbor, we can know that we are loved by God since God loved us before we loved God or neighbor, and it is only out of and because of God's love that we are able to love.

There is a sense in which these aspects of assurance—confession and love of the other—are deeply interconnected. Continual calling on God in confession is precisely a recognition and confession of the heart turned in on itself—a downplaying of the ego. In living in love toward the other, we live the realities of that confession and the forgiveness we receive from God, no longer justifying and preserving our own selves and egos but living freely for neighbors and those others God has given to us as gift.

Conclusion

Many other things could be said about the breadth of salvation.
St. Paul points us on many occasions to the cosmic and univer-
sal scope of saving grace. And then there is the issue of what we
are to make of the so-called holy pagans throughout Scripture—
Melchizedek, Jethro, Rahab, Esther, and so forth. Or there is the
question of what we are to make of the non-Jewish people who
appear in the Gospels in light of salvation—the Roman centurions,
Greeks, Samaritans, and the Syrophoenician woman. One further
and slightly more in-depth theological issue is how we see the relationship between creation, salvation, and redemption. Should we
always say that God saves and redeems because God creates? Or
might it be equally true to say that God saves and redeems, and
for this purpose God creates? Space does not allow such further
explorations, and indeed it will take us all eternity to explore the
God who is our life and salvation.

But it is still necessary to ask the question of what we are to make
of repentance in light of this picture of the breadth of salvation
that has been offered. If there are numerous images, symbols, and
understandings of salvation (chap. 1), and if the effects of salvation
should be conceived more broadly to incorporate restored human-
to-human relations (chap. 2), and if the breadth of imagination
about the scope of salvation needs to be broadened (chap. 3), what
are we to make of the call to repent and believe in the good news?
It is to this topic we now turn.

4

The Breadth of Repentance

We live today in an age when many people don't even know who Jesus is, don't know the gospel stories, don't have the Sunday school upbringing they likely would have had during a previous generation. When we talk about faith with people, witness to them, or even preach to them, we need to realize that they simply don't have the background or the basis in the faith which once was common. We live in an age when people are almost more likely to go to the gym, and certainly more likely to go to the supermarket, than to go to church on a Sunday morning. So many people have no comprehension of what it means to need Christ; there's no Christ-shaped hole of which they are aware.

It is also true that in an age of relativism and postmodern pick-and-mix approaches to life, people often don't even have the moral compass necessary to identify sins to which we might appeal as preachers. They don't know they are sick, so how do we heal them? They don't know they are lacking, so how do we give to them? How do we understand repentance, therefore, in an age when there is no social memory of Christianity? How do we speak of the need to turn from sin (in our witnessing or our preaching) when what social memory of Christianity there is often comes in the form of the inoculation to religion that we are offered in school assemblies, children's services, and childhood prayers—actions that lead us to associate the gospel with the fairy stories we were read at bedtime just after we said our prayers? And if we start to rethink this, what does it mean for the way we understand the urgency of the gospel, the seriousness of sin, the need to repent?

We live in an age when the call of the gospel—the call to repent and believe the good news—is either meaningless for people or, worse, associated with slightly eccentric street preachers wearing placards on which are written the words "The end is nigh." However, the Bible tells us that this was the root teaching of Jesus: "Jesus came to Galilee, proclaiming the good news of God, and saying, 'The time is fulfilled, and the kingdom of God has come near; repent, and believe in the good news'" (Mark 1:14–15). And so, faced with this situation, we tend normally to follow one of two options. The first option is that we ignore the idea of repentance altogether, replacing it with some rather warm and woolly idea of the love of God and acting more like social workers than disciples and workers for the kingdom of God. We do not attend to the urgency of the gospel and the significance of human response, even if that response is always vastly asymmetric to the action and saving activity of God. The second option is that we vastly overemphasize the significance of human response, understanding it in ever narrower and more formulaic ways and failing sufficiently to attend to the saving grace of God which precedes and accompanies all of our human action. In this case we focus on repentance (and often very specific under-standings of what we think that means) in such a way as to force this down people's throats. We fail to proclaim the good news of salvation, replacing it with the bad news of judgment. And we hold people at some kind of theological gunpoint, offering them hell or our own version of what we think conversion or repentance looks like. Obviously, these are the two extremes, but there is probably an element of each in large swaths of the church and all of us are likely to be somewhere on that spectrum.

Evidently, there is a problem with both approaches to repentance. With the first option, when we ignore repentance, we are confronted with the fact that Jesus himself preached this message. It was at the heart of all he was about. It seems to be at the core, the Gospels tell us, of what Jesus himself proclaimed. And evidently, some kind of human response is vitally important: the gospel is urgent; the path is narrow; the Lord calls us to turn from our sins and to a new life. But with the second option, problems exist as well. We come to feel too certain that we know exactly what repentance is and looks like in each case. And so we believe that we come to know those who have repented and that we can divide humans into two distinct categories. Moreover, in the current cultural context with its lack of social memory about what repentance might mean, or even what sin is, we struggle to proclaim salvation, and when we do, it more often than not comes out as condemnation. And then, in relation to those who came long ago to the faith, we are at a loss to know what to say, and the good news can, when repeated with bangs on the pulpit, just become old news.

But when we look at the gospel stories themselves, our focus has to shift. Gospel accounts of repentance offer a much broader, fuller, deeper sense of what repentance means than the Bible-thumping announcement of "Turn or burn" or "Die and fry." There is an interesting feature of Mark's Gospel which helps us learn what it means to preach repentance within the breadth of salvation today. Although we are told that repentance is part of the core of Jesus's proclamation (Mark 1:15) and the message Jesus comes to proclaim and is proclaiming, we never again hear the word *repent* on Jesus's lips. Either Mark gets it wrong, therefore, and this wasn't what Jesus was about; or he's recording irrelevant aspects of the ministry of Jesus in what follows since it doesn't address repentance; or (and this seems more likely) in speaking of Jesus's proclamation "Repent

and believe," Mark gives us a summary of the whole ministry of
Jesus, and what follows is an outworking of that. We might say
that "Repent and believe" is a subtitle in the Gospel of the whole
Galilean ministry of Jesus. And if we want to understand the full
breadth of repentance in the breadth of salvation, we have to look
to the ministry of the Savior.

Repentance in both its most basic and its fullest sense is at the
heart of the gospel. It is not just about the preaching of Jesus but
about his ministry in its totality. It is not some religious act which
takes place in the safe and sanitized world inside a church or a
mission tent; rather, it is the activity of turning to the Savior who
first turned toward us. For us to proclaim repentance is, in the
communities we are involved in and with the people we meet in all
of the varied ordinariness of life, to turn with the Savior who turns
to us and to all creation.

Turning to Christ

The Unsaid Aspects of the Gospel

In the last couple of years, I've become fascinated by two things
in the gospel stories. The first is that not everyone becomes a disciple. We have the calling of the first disciples in Mark 1:16–20,
and there are others. But only a few people ever become disciples.
Other people whom Jesus meets and ministers to don't turn to
Christ in this way. There are all kinds of people who respond to
his ministry and proclamation of repentance and do not become
disciples but go back to their everyday lives, transformed by this
amazing encounter with the Holy One of God. We need to be
open to the fact that many people will in profound ways have
met Jesus but never become disciples—living lives like before but
transformed by an encounter with the Saving One. And our role in
the church, even before we seek to make disciples of every nation,

is to allow people to turn to Christ in all kinds of ways—just as they did in the gospel stories.

The second thing I am fascinated by is that the stories of the gospel are rarely resolved. We don't get "happily ever after" endings with all the details tied up. We are not told that everyone changed their lives completely and set up a church in the area they lived in, and we should neither presume this nor read it into what the gospel offers us. Rather, we are told simply that people met Jesus in a profound way, and maybe they just returned to their ordinary lives. The focus is always on the encounter with Jesus—on the Saving One, not the saved. There's a real artistic tendency at the moment in film and drama to leave stories open-ended and not to complete the full details of the narrative, leaving the viewer to guess (and perhaps a little uncomfortable—at least if they are an instinctive completer-finisher as I am!). The gospel is full of the same kinds of narratives in which we get tiny glimpses into lives transformed, and we rarely (if ever) know the full narrative and the ending. I don't think we are wise to make these up.

Reconceiving Repentance

In connection with this, I want to suggest that we need a broader and a more biblical understanding of what it is to repent: it is, primarily, to *turn toward Christ*. When I was a doctoral student, I took it upon myself to read all ten-million-plus words of the theologian Karl Barth's writings. It was a rich blessing to have the time to do it. But I have to say it was a slog at various points, and easy for the pages to blur into one another. One of the moments when I woke up from my haze of wading through it, though, was when I read Barth's claim that Jesus Christ makes us into sinners. It stood out to me and shocked me. How could this be true? But the more I pondered it, the more it seemed to me absolutely right for our age and generation. People don't have a compass of sin anymore. Telling people they are sinners who need to repent doesn't work when they have no sense of the law under which they are condemned and have failed. Furthermore, I am not sure that repentance means, in the first instance, turning from sin. After all, we can turn from a life of sin in all kinds of directions—turning toward Buddhism or compassionate humanism, and so forth. It's not that first we turn from sin and in doing so we turn to Christ. It is the opposite way around: we turn toward Christ and—as a by-product almost—we turn from our sin. Crucially, we do not need first to be turned into sinners who acknowledge their fallenness before we can know the gospel. That is never what happens in the gospel accounts. People turn to Jesus first: he allows them to come to him in their sin. Indeed, it is only in meeting with Jesus Christ, knowing his standard and his call, that we begin to understand the ways in which we fall short of his perfect humanity—what it means to sin. Only when we know Christ can we begin to know what it means to be a sinner and fall on our knees in repentance. In an age of no collective social memory of the gospel, we need first to enable people to be confronted with Christ to know him, and to focus on telling people about *him* so they can repent—that is, so they can turn toward him.

Indeed, this was the heart of the gospel account for those who heard these stories for the first time. The call of Christ to repentance is first of all a call to turn to him. It is the turning toward Christ that is the first and crucial aspect of repentance. What we turn away from results from our turning to him and takes a lifetime of repentance to work out. People in the Gospels turn to Christ in all kinds of contexts and from all kinds of things. Space prohibits a full account of each of the narratives of the gospel's message of repenting in turning to Christ, but in offering a few of these in what follows, I hope to impart a flavor of them to help us read Scripture in a way which is practical and assists us in our witness and mission in the world. We need a way of recognizing the gospel as the living voice of Jesus addressing us in the contexts and the world we find ourselves in. We need a way of joining in Jesus's ministry of calling people to repentance through the lives we lead as Christians.

Turning Helplessly

In Mark 1:29–34, very soon after we are told of the ministry of repentance in which Jesus was engaged in Galilee, we are told the story of Jesus healing Simon's mother-in-law, who was in bed with a fever. At first glance it doesn't look like a story of repentance, but it is. It is a story in which—even in her illness and her incapacity to respond to Jesus—Jesus turns to her, and because he has turned to her, she responds by turning to him and serving him.

Until only a year or so ago I had always enjoyed good health, for which I was grateful. But this last year I have struggled with very serious asthma, which has, in turn, led to my getting more infections and to being much more tired than I usually am. Although I am OK, I have at times felt utterly helpless in light of physical illness; it has been a shock to me. But to have had a fever in bed in the ancient world—before the onset of modern medicine—would have been an altogether more debilitating and life-threatening issue. Simon's mother-in-law must have been drained of life and vitality, since we are told that Jesus "lifted her up" (Mark 1:31). Like this woman whom Jesus had to take by the hand and raise up, so many people at some point in their lives find themselves in situations of physical dependency and helplessness. This story is a story of repentance in utter helplessness—of turning to Jesus in our moments of almost unconscious and passive desperation and need. It is a story of how we can turn to Jesus (repent) at these times since we are able (like Simon's mother-in-law) to turn to Jesus because Jesus turns first to us.

Turning to Jesus for Others

In the gospel stories, repentance sometimes results when people turn to Jesus for the sake of someone else. If we look at Mark 1:30

carefully, it's clear that it is others who turn to Jesus for Peter's mother-in-law. After all, how could she, when she was in bed with a fever? "Now Simon's mother-in-law was in bed with a fever, and *they* told him about her at once." It is on account of the intercession of other people, who themselves turn to Jesus, that Jesus turns to Simon's mother-in-law. It is they who tell him about her. (We get this point also in Mark 2 with the story of the paralytic who is carried to Jesus by friends.) Through the intercession of others who turn to Jesus, Jesus turns to Peter's mother-in-law and she is able to turn to him.

This is a tremendous confirmation of the importance of prayer. What Simon and Andrew and James and John do is essentially the same as what we do when we pray for someone. And while Jesus may not be physically present now, when we pray to him for others, we are doing what these disciples did: we are turning to Christ, asking him to turn to those we love and who need him, so that they can turn to him through his salvation. We can ask Jesus to turn to people, especially if they cannot for whatever reason turn to him. We can ask Jesus to turn to people when they themselves are helpless.

In salvation, we are all helpless in our own efforts to turn to Christ; it is only the Spirit's prevenient grace which frees us to do so. But when we see others who are suffering and we feel unable to help, that can feel particularly painful. When we see them lost and in darkness, we often feel helpless in knowing what to do. The same is also true when we face people whom we love whose physical helplessness we cannot aid. We feel at a loss to know what to do. We ourselves feel helpless at someone else's helplessness. And sometimes we even come to feel like we are part of the problem. Going through my mum having cancer was very much like that. But I was struck by this all the more when I watched my mum deal only a couple of years later with her own mother going through the same illness. In many ways, my own mum coped better when she was ill than when she found herself unable to help her own mother who was ill. Being unable to help someone who is helpless is at times even more painful than being helpless oneself.

These disciples find themselves in that position of helplessness. And they do the only thing they can: they *turn* to Jesus. They turn to him because they have hope that he is the one who can help in even the most helpless of situations. They implore him to do what no one else can. We might say they engage in intercession.

Jesus Turns to the Helpless

Turning to the disciples who turn to him in their helplessness and need, Jesus turns to Peter's mother-in-law. He takes her by the hand (even though she has not asked him to) and raises her up, and she is restored to health. She is saved. If repentance is really at its core and root about turning to Jesus, what then are we to make of Jesus turning to someone who is unable to turn to him? I am very taken by this image. This woman does not ask him; she is not, it seems, free to choose what he offers. Jesus just sees her there, helpless in her need, gripped by fever; and he takes her by the hand and lifts her up. He turns to her in compassion.

So often, so much of our talk about salvation places such a priority on people turning to God. It places so much on *choosing* the Christian faith. It places so much on us as human beings and our responsibility in the grand vista of divine salvation. This passage is a challenge to that—as, indeed, much of the gospel is. It is not, in the end, the woman's desire to follow Jesus, or the fact she has prayed "the sinner's prayer," or the fact she has converted, or the fact she has been baptized and has shared in the church's sacraments, or the fact she has become a member of a church community that leads Jesus to turn to her. It is instead because some other people ask him, and he—in his immeasurable, free love and compassion—turns to her. There is nothing about free choice in this for the mother-in-law; there is nothing about decisions of the heart or of the mind for her. This is simply and utterly and completely Jesus: he turns to her when she can't turn to him.

Healings are stories of salvation. Salvation means, I suppose, restoration. Healings are about a restoration (a salvation) to health. The healing stories tell us about Jesus's desire to restore people, to save people—literally often from death. So often we think salvation takes place in a set-piece, formulaic way which we understand and can observe. Jesus's love and compassion are greater than all that. He doesn't just turn to us when we are able to help ourselves and willfully to turn to him. He helps us in our helplessness. He turns to us in our need.

Let us remember such stories when we are tempted to draw lines of distinction between types of people and to make absolute judgments about believers and unbelievers. How many unknown millions has Jesus turned to in their helplessness? How many silent prayers of loved ones have been responded to by Jesus holding the hands of the sick and dying? How many unknown and untold prayers have been made by those lying down and unable to speak? How many of these has Jesus taken by the hand and raised to his salvation?

When I think with sorrow of the millions who die alone, or who are helpless, or who are sick, I am comforted by this image—the image of a Savior who turns to us in our need and holds our hand. He doesn't just command the illness to be gone, or make a decree (as we know from elsewhere in the gospel narratives he can). Instead, he takes time to hold her by the hand even when she can ask nothing of him. Whether we are able to ask him to or not, Jesus, who turns to us in compassion, is there with us. I am confident that Jesus finds a way to hold the hands of the sick and dying, that he answers the prayers of helpless relatives who look on, that he raises the dying to his salvation and eternal life. And in turning to them in their helplessness, he finds a way for genuine repentance, genuine turning to him, to happen. And this happens without great scenes, and probably we are unaware, but it happens.

My maternal grandfather was not a good man. He was a criminal and spent time in prison. He drank and was involved with drugs. He and my grandmother had divorced when my mother (the kindest soul you could meet) was a toddler. Neither my mother nor I had any real relationship with her father. But when he had grown old, as he lay there dying, with just my father in the room, my dad spoke the gospel to him and prayed. Who knows what happened? My grandfather never woke up. He never prayed a prayer aloud. He never responded in a way we could see. But I am confident that Jesus was holding him by the hand and giving him every opportunity to allow Christ to raise him up to his saving and redeeming life. And—while there are so many broken parts of the story of his life and certainly his relationships with us—it would not surprise me if one day we are restored and reconciled in a context of confession and forgiveness and redeeming grace in the Lord's own kingdom.

The Helpless Turn to Jesus

For this woman in the story in Mark, however, there is a chance to respond to Jesus in this life. Jesus turns to her in her need and helplessness. He brings salvation to her in her passivity. But in the end there is a miracle, and she is made well. And her *response* to Jesus's turning to her in grace and love and compassion is that she *serves* him and his disciples (Mark 1:31). She is cured, and her response is one of service. She turns to Jesus, who turned first to her. So often we put the primary and active element of repentance onto the human: repentance becomes *our* act which *we choose* to engage in. That is not the case here. The woman turns to Jesus *in response* to his turning first to her. Her repentance is responsive: she turns, having been turned to. In every form, repentance is always a response to the one who, while we were still sinners, died for us (Rom. 5:8). Our turning to Christ is always a response to the one who turns to us.

We do not know what miracles happen in individual people's lives—how they are helped out by God and how they quietly attend to serving him as a response to that. Simon's mother-in-law never becomes one of the Twelve. She's probably just a nice older woman who works in the house. What is important is that Jesus turned to her when she was helpless, and she responded by simply serving him and his followers in the normal ways of her life. If ever we need an image of salvation, it is here.

Turning to Outcasts

When I was in Russia a few years ago, I went to a theater in St. Petersburg with a friend of mine from England. It was freezing cold, and we were wrapped up in coats and hats and overtrousers. My friend, who is six foot five and bald, looked like some kind of Bond film baddie, dressed in a snowsuit. We arrived at the theater in plenty of time, sat down, and waited for the show to begin. Just as it was about to start, a young couple took their seats behind us. The gentleman's seat was directly behind my friend's. As he took his place, he announced in English rather loudly to his wife, "Trust me to be sat behind the giant Russian freak!" My friend turned around and said, "I might be a giant freak, but I'm an English one, not a Russian one!"

The man had assumed that since we were surrounded by Russians and in Russia, we too must be Russian. He had drawn conclusions about us as individuals from the community we found ourselves a part of, even just on that one evening. Who we choose to mix with says a lot about us, and people jump to conclusions by the company we keep. In some ways this is natural. No human being can exist alone. We are born to someone; we operate as members of a community; we are forced to interact with others in society.

The problem with groups is that they can become exclusive, and we exclude people because of what others might think about us.

Isn't that how every fancy golf club or country club operates? If people jump to conclusions about us and make judgments about us, we have to be careful about the company we keep. But we need to be careful of placing an exclusivity on Jesus's proclamation of the kingdom and those whom it involves. This is not to say that anything goes: behavior needs to be challenged, and those whose behavior is excluding or abusive need to be challenged. But it is to say that the call to belief and repentance, the challenge of the kingdom of God, applies to all and involves all. This is a kingdom which has no end—a kingdom which does not define itself by an exclusive sense of identity but by a radical inclusivity. And this powerful inclusivity again shows us the breadth of repentance: it tells of the Jesus who turns to the outcasts and the outcasts who turn to Jesus, and the community that is built and restored in that.

Jesus Turns to the Outsider

The remarkable aspect of two passages at the start of Mark's Gospel resides in their capacity to show us what it means for Jesus to turn to those who lie outside the "normal" or "acceptable" people with whom one might form community. His openness to a leper (Mark 1:40–45) and to tax collectors and sinners (Mark 2:15–17) demonstrates a freedom that Jesus has in his self-identity. Not needing to be defined *by* others and the status they think they have (which is meaningless in light of the only begotten Son of God!), Jesus's humanity is defined in his identity as one *for* others. Unafraid of what others might think of him and the exclusion this might (and indeed did) bring for him, Jesus turns to the leper and the sinners and tax collectors in a manner which *includes* them. He turns to them in a way which allows them to turn to him. He turns to them in a manner which recognizes their humanity alongside his own, and in his own humanity he is moved with compassion to give them full human dignity. This inclusion is illustrated in two groups of people.

The first of these is represented by the leper of Mark 1:40–45. In this story we see an overcoming of social exclusion. The leper comes up to Jesus, pleading with him to heal him. This story has a number of remarkable features. The first is that Jesus did not run away. Leprosy is contagious, and contact with lepers was considered highly dangerous. Lepers, indeed, needed to wear bells around their necks to warn people they were coming so they could make their getaway. Lepers were avoided—removed from normal society, living in their own communities outside the city often in terrible conditions, excluded from the rest of the people and all forms of social interaction. For Jesus simply to have allowed a leper to approach him is a truly remarkable thing.

Furthermore, Jesus's reaction to this was not awkwardness or a desire to escape the situation as soon as possible. Instead, his reaction was that of pity (v. 41). And this pity was a pity which moved Jesus to stretch out his hand and touch the leper. To engage in such an action was clearly dangerous; to those around it must have seemed that Jesus himself was running the risk of catching leprosy. That Jesus chose to heal the leper in such a way speaks volumes for the radical inclusivity and humanizing salvation present in his kingdom. No doubt Jesus could have chosen to make the leper clean in another way—simply saying the words or allowing him to touch his robe (as the woman with the hemorrhage did). Instead, Jesus stretched out his hand to touch the leper. He made it clear that he was welcome and part of his community. The act of touch was an act of inclusion for the leper.

What is more, to have engaged in such an action shows that Jesus did not think of his own status or his own need for social inclusion. In allowing the leper to approach him, in touching the leper, Jesus too ran the risk of being excluded from society. Prepared to risk catching leprosy and becoming a scandal in society, Jesus engages in this radical and radically inclusive action. He includes even when this inclusion could lead to his exclusion. And in including the leper, in reaching out to touch him, Jesus makes the leper clean and heals him. He turns to the leper in his dehumanized status as an outcast and touches him, allowing him to turn to Jesus and become part of his people.

The second type of people that Jesus includes is present in Mark 2:15–17. These are the moral outcasts, represented in the characters of the sinners and the tax collectors. Here the scandal that Jesus causes is clearly recorded by Mark. The Pharisees are perplexed and troubled as to why Jesus eats with sinners and tax collectors. They feel this says something about him as a person. Yet the sinners and the tax collectors are welcome at Jesus's table. His radical inclusivity does not stretch only to those who have no ability to control their exclusion and who through no fault of their own are excluded (as in the case of the leper). Jesus's radical inclusivity involves turning even to those who are judged to be morally deficient as a result of the wrongful exercise of their free will.

Tax collectors were hated figures in Judea. They represented Roman authority and governance; they worked for the occupiers, taking money from the local people for the Roman treasury and growing rich themselves in the process. These figures are combined with the "sinners"—probably figures who were notorious in their flouting of the written law in contrast to the Pharisees, who adhered strictly to the written law and believed the oral law had to be followed with equally strict adherence. Sinners and tax collectors were religious, moral, and thereby social outcasts.

It is these that Jesus shares table fellowship with. These are the people invited to dinner with him. Jesus identifies himself with those who willfully excluded themselves through their sin or willingness to cooperate with the occupying forces for the sake of making money. If a person is defined in some way by the company he keeps, we must ask what this would have said about Jesus. It says something about the fact that his kingdom does have a place for such people, that they are welcome at his table, that they are the people to whom he calls (Mark 2:17).

The Outsider Turns to Jesus

By turning to the outsiders, Jesus allows the outsiders to turn to him. He turns to them and they turn to him. He shows us what repentance looks like. Jesus's own words in Mark 2:17, "I have come to call not the righteous but sinners," demonstrate the purpose of his mission and ministry. He comes not primarily for those who have found God but for those who need to be called to God. In this, *he* is the active subject; *he* is the one who takes the initiative. The crowds, which include sinners and tax collectors, follow him; but he calls the sinners, the outcasts, and he invites them to eat with him. No doubt Jesus could have just eaten with his disciples, or with the "acceptable" people who were following him; but his decision was to dine not only with his disciples but also with the hated outcasts. He recognizes their humanity; he sees that they too are the precious children of God. We can only imagine the effect of that on these judged and condemned and excluded people: "Here is this holy man, this man who has performed miraculous works, this man who has claimed the authority to forgive sins, and here he is inviting me, a sinner, to sit at the table with him and eat."

What is more, this was a meal quite possibly at Jesus's own house. It seems that the "his" in the Greek of Mark 2:15 may well refer to Jesus rather than to Levi; Levi is not mentioned in the original language. If Jesus himself was the host, this would better explain the outrage and horror of the Pharisees at his eating with moral outcasts. These people were being welcomed into Jesus's own home. Were that not enough, they were being welcomed to a special meal. Again, the Greek in verse 15 reveals that the diners were reclining to eat. This was not a normal practice but one reserved for solemn meals or when guests were being entertained in style. These guests were being lavishly treated by their host; this was a big and a special occasion. Jesus had turned to the sinners and the outcasts and had welcomed them into his own home for a feast. This is like the scene

in Victor Hugo's book *Les Misérables* in which the bishop welcomes
the escaped convict Jean Valjean to eat with him at his house. Rather
than simply giving him leftovers and letting him eat in the kitchen
with the cook, the bishop lays the table with the best silver he has
and recognizes this destitute man as his honored guest and a child
of God. Similarly and more powerfully, Jesus (who is God incarnate)
turns to these outcasts and invites them in to eat with him. He turns
to them so that they may turn to him to be healed, for he came to
heal not the well but those in need of a physician (Mark 2:17). He
invites them to his home to feast with him, and they accept. They
repent. They turn to him.

In the case of the leper, it may seem that Jesus is more passive.
The leper seems to do all the chasing; it is he who approaches Jesus,
begging and kneeling and pleading to be made clean. But Jesus does
turn to him; he turns to him and touches him and makes him well.
Jesus could have turned away but doesn't. He turns to this sick man;
the Great Physician cures him. Unless Jesus had turned to him, the
leper would have remained an outsider. Unless Jesus had healed
him, he would not have been included. It is Jesus's willingness to
turn to outsiders and to welcome them in that is the key criterion
for the inclusion of outsiders. Without turning to them, it could
never happen: the leper would still be a leper; the leper would still
have no community.

This is where we begin to see our role as the church in proclaiming, "Repent and believe the good news." The outsider can never turn
to Christ unless we turn first to the outsider with Christ. St. Paul
puts this well in Romans 10:14–15:

> But how are they to call on one in whom they have not believed?
> And how are they to believe in one of whom they have never heard?
> And how are they to hear without someone to proclaim him? And
> how are they to proclaim him unless they are sent? As it is written,
> "How beautiful are the feet of those who bring good news!"

We are called to bring good news to the sinner and the outcast and the prisoner and the brokenhearted and the sick and the dying—news which is so good that even the feet of the one proclaiming it are beautiful. Jesus could have ignored the leper; instead, he touched and healed him. Jesus could have could have eaten with religious people and dignitaries; instead, he ate with sinners and tax collectors. He turned to those who needed him even though they were outcasts, and he made them welcome. He turned to those who were outsiders and made them insiders. And what is more, he turned to them while they were still outsiders. He touched the leper while he was a leper, not after he healed him; he did not wait for the sinners and tax collectors to reform from their sin before inviting them in to eat with him. The outsiders do not have to become socially, morally, religiously, or physically acceptable before Jesus turns to them. The same must be true for us as the church. It is to these people that the church must turn, not in judgment but in hospitality, with the *good news* of repentance and the kingdom of God. This good news is that the King has already turned to us to bring us with him to the kingdom; we just need to join him. We must not wait for others to reform or change before we offer them a place at our Lord's table; he did not do that. But we must recognize that they can never call on Jesus if they have not believed, and cannot believe if they have not heard, and cannot hear unless someone tells them—unless someone turns to them as outsiders and tells them that as they are, they belong inside the kingdom of our God.

This is not to say that anything goes. The leper is still a leper when he comes to Jesus; the sinners and tax collectors are sick in another way. Both sets of people need healing. But it is to say that they have a place to be welcomed into God's kingdom—a place where healing and transformation may *begin*. We should not imagine that we need to be transformed before sitting at the table, or before meeting Jesus. Sitting at the table and meeting Jesus is the transformation.

That is the repentance. It marks the start of transformation, not the end point.

Who Are the Insiders?

In fact, there is a great irony in this issue of who the outcasts are. Reading the passage from Mark 2:15–17, one is left asking the question, Who are the insiders? Jesus has proclaimed that the kingdom of God is at hand (Mark 1:14), and we begin to realize who the members of this kingdom are. Mark has told us in the very first verse of his Gospel that he is writing about the good news of Jesus Christ, the Son of God. And we might well imagine that this good news is for those we would think the Son of God would want to mix with—those we understand as the holy, the righteous, the religious, the acceptable, the elite, the insiders. We might well imagine that these are the people who have a place in his kingdom. As the story unfolds, however, we recognize that this is not so. The insiders in this kingdom include the outsiders in social and religious terms. They include the lepers and the sinners and the tax collectors. And the latter two categories are invited inside Jesus's own house. There is a complete reinterpretation of who the insiders are.

This comes, however, with a further challenging question: Who are the outsiders? The challenge comes when we begin to realize that it is not only that the category of insiders is redefined, but that the category of outsiders is redefined also. The Pharisees do not seem to be on the inside at all. They were extremely pious and committed religious people. They were highly observant of Torah (the law) and the other taught obligations that the most religious were to take part in. They were, in a sense, the religious superclass of their age—perhaps akin to extremely committed fundamentalists of differing kinds in our own generation. One might imagine that their commitment and passion would see them as the ones right at the center of the inside with Jesus, deep, deep within—even if others were allowed in at the fringes. But this is not so. Scandalized that Jesus is eating with sinners and tax collectors, they clearly will not eat with Jesus because of the company he is keeping. Because of the others Jesus welcomes to the inside, they have removed themselves and placed themselves on the outside.

An inversion has taken place: the religious and the morally and socially acceptable have become outsiders because they cannot be insiders alongside the others whom Jesus has welcomed to his table. Even though they live lives supposedly turned away from sin, they fail to repent, because they cannot turn to Jesus because of whose company he keeps. This is a deep challenge. When we seek to exclude those we see to be the outsiders, it is we who become the outsiders, we who become the unrepentant. We have no place at the table of our Lord unless we realize there is a place for all.

It may well be that we do not feel so clearly like the Pharisees. We may not be those who consciously exclude. Instead, we may think of ourselves more like Jesus's disciples. We are happy for there to be others at the table, as long as they recognize that we are in the central position as those who are the primary concern of Jesus. But even to those of us who identify with this camp, there is a significant challenge. The disciples appear to take a secondary place to the sinners and tax collectors. It is not that they occupy the primary place and the sinners and tax collectors a secondary one. Almost the reverse is true: Jesus is prepared to scandalize (to affect their standing) the disciples in order to eat with the sinners and tax collectors. The disciples are present, but it is not really a story about them; it is a story about Jesus eating with sinners and tax collectors. The disciples seem incidental to the story in many ways; the message of the story would not change without them. Their place is different from that of the sinners and tax collectors (the disciples are given the particular name "disciple"), but it does not seem a privileged position. It is not that Jesus eats with the disciples and that the sinners and tax collectors are allowed to watch or are invited in for dessert or a drink afterward. The outcasts are fully present in the same way the disciples are, not simply fringe members.

There is a challenge here for the church. The presence of the modern-day outcast, the modern-day sinner and tax collector, in our church reminds us of the presence of Christ, without whom and without whose grace and forgiveness all of us are sinners or tax collectors. The outcasts are a gift to us. It is not that, as modern-day disciples, we should put up with such people and merely tolerate them; it is that we must welcome them to our Lord's table because in God's house all are welcomed, as *Christ* brings us in and sits us down to eat with him, to feast with him. None of us has a particular status or standing that affords us rights at the table beyond our willingness (in all of the mess of each of our lives) to turn to Jesus. The sinners and tax collectors of today are not to be smuggled through back doors and tradesmen's entrances. They are to be welcomed with the warm shaking of hands, escorted into the celebration, and made to recognize that they are at home where we want them to feast since the church is no one's house but God's, and in God's house all are welcome.

As the modern Pharisees that we so often can be, we must turn from looking in on ourselves and on others like us to looking outward to those human beings we recognize perhaps with fear—fear of the pollution of our own group, fear of what others might think of us, fear of finding something of ourselves in these seemingly dangerous others. In that turning outward, the righteous recognize that they themselves are righteous only as they have been turned to face Christ (only as they have repented in looking toward him), and in facing Christ they must face the others to whom Christ turns in his grace and love. The church must turn to these others, not as interlopers into the celebration, but as treasured guests of our Lord who deserve to be welcomed with gladness and joy to his table, and served by us as they sit with him.

The Response to Inclusion

The effect of this bringing of the outsider to the inside must never be underestimated. We see this in the story of the leper who is healed. While the story of the sinners and tax collectors ends with the way in which Jesus was judged for the company he kept, the story of the leper ends from the perspective of the leper who was an outsider and was brought within. Here is a man with leprosy who would have been excluded almost entirely from normal society, and he is healed. More than that, he is healed by Jesus actually touching him. What a reaction we see! After Jesus instructs him to make the correct sacrifice and warns him not to tell anyone what had happened, Mark tells us this: "But he went out and began to proclaim it freely, and to spread the word, so that Jesus could no longer go into a town openly, but stayed out in the country; and people came to him from every quarter" (Mark 1:45). But could we expect anything else? The man cannot contain what has happened to him. He spreads the word so freely that Jesus can no longer move openly in the towns and has to withdraw to the countryside. But even there the people follow him from every quarter.

The man who had leprosy was sternly warned not to tell anyone what Jesus had done (Mark 1:43–44). Are we to condemn him for this action? Our response to this question must surely be no. Secrecy is a broader theme in Mark's Gospel, and this detail is part of that. But, at one level at least, this detail serves to demonstrate the enormous impact that the transformation had on the man. He simply could not contain what Jesus had done for him. His action was not one of willful disobedience to Jesus. Rather, it was the action of one who was so overcome with joy and delight that he could do nothing but tell everyone he met what had happened to him. The only action he could undertake was to spread the message freely. He could not contain it.

It is difficult to imagine what it would be like to find oneself included after being excluded in such a powerful way for so long.

The leper's inability to keep it to himself demonstrates the profound nature of his inclusion. To live without community is a dreadful thing. In a sense, it is part of what we do to prisoners in depriving them of their freedom: they are deprived the freedom of forming community other than with those foist on them by similar circumstance. The leper was in some ways a prisoner to his own exclusion. And freed from that exclusion, how does he respond? He goes to people to tell them what Jesus has done. We should not miss this aspect of the story. The man would have been unable to go up to people when he was a leper. He would have been unable to enter into a habitation, and the law commanded that if a leper approached, the leper was to cry, "Unclean!" (Lev. 13:45–46). The sense of solitude, rejection, and exclusion is unimaginable. The leper responds to his healing by telling people, by engaging in human interaction. He demonstrates the desire and need for community and the joy and rejoicing that come with inclusion. He is now able to approach people, to speak with them, to be a social creature—to be fully human, living like Christ fully for God and fully for others. And his first act of engagement with others is to tell them what has happened to him, and of this Jesus whom he turned to, who turned to him, touched him, and made him well—who included him. His response is to proclaim the reality of the breadth of repentance within redeeming and saving grace.

How wonderful it would be if the church grasped just some of this radical inclusivity, some of the power of the breadth of the meaning of repentance! If we did, there would be many who would have the response of the leper. Each of them would bring the many they cannot but tell, as the leper did, who would in turn bring many, who would in turn bring many. Revival will not come by emphasizing sin, by condemning people, by calling out the problems in their lives, by being puritanical and separatist, by judging, by pointing to all that people have done wrong, by preaching bad news. Revival will come only by emphasizing Christ and being as welcoming and inclusive as he was, that all may turn to him. Revival will come when we recognize that each one of us can only come to Christ "just as I am, without one plea." Only in recognizing that we too are outsiders except by the grace of Jesus in turning to us, and that we too, therefore, are sinners and tax collectors, lepers and outcasts, can we begin to realize the hospitality of our Lord and the joy we must feel in being a part of his kingdom. This needs to be our preaching of repentance: we need to turn to all kinds of people with Christ, just as they are; allow them to turn to him, just as they are; and then allow him, through his Spirit, to transform them from who they are in sin to who they are eternally destined to be in him. Repentance is not about setting conditions on the gospel. Repentance is about proclaiming the gospel in all its breadth.

Conclusion

These are just two small examples of the breadth of repentance in the Gospel narratives. Throughout each of the Gospels, there is story after story of those to whom Jesus turns and those who turn to Jesus. Of course, we see the disciples turning to Christ to follow him. But we also see, at the other end of the spectrum, the demoniacs turning to Christ in anger and fear and captivity. We see the paralytic turning to Christ through friends. We see the crowds of four and five thousand turning to Christ in hunger. We see Mary Magdalene turning to Christ in the garden in confusion. We see the rich young ruler turning to Christ for advice. And on and on it goes. How many people turn to Christ (repent) in all kinds of ways which don't fit our ecclesiastical norms? How many people do we think are outside when actually Jesus has turned to them and they to Jesus in all kinds of unknown, quiet, yet transformative ways?

As the church, we are to share in the ministry of calling the world to repentance. But that means calling the world to turn to Christ first. And when they turn to Christ—in whatever way and situation and context and manner—then they will begin to turn away from sin and death and hell. We are never to call them *into* sin and death and hell, believing that by proclaiming repentance we are able to rescue them from sin, death, and hell. Christ turns to all creation in grace. We need to help people find him in their lives in all of their complexities and differences—to discover him already there at work in and for them. And in so doing, we will grasp something of the vast breadth of repentance within the unending heights and depths of salvation. In so doing, we proclaim good news. In so doing, we proclaim Christ, who is the King and brings the kingdom, which is so near that it is almost in touching distance.

Conclusion

Salvation is at once infinitely simpler than we often make it and infinitely greater than we can imagine. It is infinitely simpler since salvation has a name, and that name is Jesus, the Savior. Salvation is all about him who leads us back to the Father through the Holy Spirit, whom he with his Father sends. Rather than being in some ornate formula or complex mechanism in which Jesus takes a part, salvation is in him; in fact, salvation *is him*. He is the God of our salvation. He is the God of the gospel. He is the Lamb to whom salvation belongs (Rev. 7:10). He is the one in whom we abide, the one in whom there is eternal life, the one whose body we have become members of, the one who turns to us in our need, the one who left the glories of heaven to become a servant, the one who saves us by manger and cross, the one who is alive and sits at the right hand ever interceding for us. Salvation comes from the Savior—the Savior who meets us by his Spirit in the breadth of our human existence in creation. Salvation comes in our turning to him who always first turns to us.

But salvation is simultaneously unimaginably greater than we can ever begin to comprehend. Salvation is not just the eternal life we receive in God's kingdom; it is also the abundant and reconciling life we receive today. It is not confined to those moments of mountaintop clarity but also follows us to the places in which we dwell in the valley of the shadow of death. It is not only the possession of those few we visibly identify, but is also for those many whom God sees, since God sees not as we see but sees instead the heart. It is to be found not only in our restored relationships with God but also in our ministry of reconciling ourselves with each other and all creation through the Spirit. It is present not only in those we see turning to God in repentance and discipleship but in all—in whatever need and place and form—who turn and call on the Lord (Acts 2:21) in their desperate or silent cry. In the end, salvation is infinitely greater than our minds can understand because it is found in the God of our salvation who is Alpha and Omega, the Creator and Lord of all the universe, the eternal and majestic I AM. It will take all eternity to know the depths of the infinite plenitude of God's being.

Rather than formulate, conceptualize, or mechanize salvation; rather than make judgments that belong to God alone; and rather than create sinners so that they know they need to repent, let us just take people to the King who possesses the kingdom and the power and glory. Let us take them to the Rock of our salvation. Instead of formulating complex theories, we are surely better off saying, with the psalmist,

> O come, let us sing to the LORD;
>> let us make a joyful noise to the rock of our salvation!
> Let us come into his presence with thanksgiving;
>> let us make a joyful noise to him with songs of praise!
> For the LORD is a great God,
>> and a great King above all gods.
> In his hand are the depths of the earth;
>> the heights of the mountains are his also.
> The sea is his, for he made it,
>> and the dry land, which his hands have formed.

> O come, let us worship and bow down,
>> let us kneel before the LORD, our Maker! (Ps. 95:1–6)

Let us sing our salvation and make a joyful noise to the God of our salvation, who holds the mountains and the valleys and the seas and the lands in God's hand. Let us worship God for the breadth of salvation. Let us behold the shining and blinding glories of God's grace. In so doing, we could do worse than join in the words of Charles Wesley's hymn "And Can It Be?"

> 'Tis mystery all! Th' Immortal dies!
> Who can explore His strange design?
> In vain the firstborn seraph tries
> To sound the depths of love divine!
> 'Tis mercy all! let earth adore,
> Let angel minds inquire no more.

> He left His Father's throne above,
> So free, so infinite His grace;
> Emptied Himself of all but love,
> And bled for Adam's helpless race;
> 'Tis mercy all, immense and free;
> For, O my God, it found out me.[1]

Let us all sing and swim and rejoice in the infinity of grace, the boundless depths of love, the mystery of the salvation of creation.

Notes

Introduction

1. I have made the decision to use non-gender-specific pronouns for God. The Christian God is neither male nor female, nor a "thing" like any other thing in creation. God is *God*. Hence, despite the fact that it might seem somewhat awkward at points, I do not use "he" or "him" for God. For too long, Christianity has replicated the patriarchalism of the culture; and for too long, we have failed to allow God to be *God*. I hope this gesture will make a small difference to such failings.

2. Translation by William Edwards (1884–1929).

Chapter 1 The Breadth of the Cross

1. Translation taken from the 1979 Book of Common Prayer.

2. For an overview of the new perspective on Paul, see James D. G. Dunn, *The New Perspective on Paul* (Grand Rapids: Eerdmans, 2005); and (on a more popular level) N. T. Wright, *What Saint Paul Really Said* (Oxford: Lion, 1997).

3. See C. H. Dodd, *The Bible and the Greeks* (London: Hodder & Stoughton, 1935), chap. 5.

4. See Philip G. Ziegler, *Militant Grace: The Apocalyptic Turn and the Future of Christian Theology* (Grand Rapids: Baker Academic, 2018).

5. See Brian Davies and G. R. Evans, eds., *Anselm of Canterbury: The Major Works* (Oxford: Oxford University Press, 1998).

6. Martin Luther, *Luther's Works*, vol. 31, *The Career of the Reformer I*, ed. Harold J. Grimm (Minneapolis: Fortress, 1958), 40.

7. These articles can be found in *The Book of Concord: The Confessions of the Evangelical Lutheran Church*, ed. Robert Kolb and Timothy J. Wengert (Minneapolis: Augsburg Fortress, 2000). The quotation is taken from p. 301.

8. See Martin Luther, *Luther's Works*, vol. 35, *Word and Sacrament I*, ed. E. Theodore Bachmann (Minneapolis: Fortress, 1959), 370.

9. See Gustaf Aulén, *Christus Victor: An Historical Study of the Three Main Types of the Idea of the Atonement* (London: SPCK, 1970).

10. The best place to find an account of Abelard's soteriology is his *Commentary on the Epistle to the Romans*, trans. Steven R. Cartwright, Fathers of the Church (Washington, DC: Catholic University Press, 2011).

11. On Schleiermacher on the atonement, see Friedrich Schleiermacher, *The Christian Faith* (Edinburgh: T&T Clark, 1968), 425–532; and on Ritschl, see Albrecht Ritschl, *The Christian Doctrine of Justification and Reconciliation* (Edinburgh: T&T Clark, 1900).

12. Abelard, "Exposition of the Epistle to the Romans," in *A Scholastic Miscellany: Anselm to Ockham*, ed. E. R. Fairweather, trans. G. E. Moffatt (Philadelphia: Westminster, 1956), 283.

Chapter 2 The Breadth of Salvation in the Society of God

1. Tom Greggs, *Dogmatic Ecclesiology*, vol. 1, *The Priestly Catholicity of the Church* (Grand Rapids: Baker Academic, 2019).

2. Yves Congar, *I Believe in the Holy Spirit*, 3 vols. (London: Geoffrey Chapman, 1983), 1:31.

3. Dietrich Bonhoeffer, *Act and Being: Transcendental Philosophy and Ontology in Systematic Theology* (Minneapolis: Fortress, 1996), 114.

4. Dietrich Bonhoeffer, *Sanctorum Communio: A Theological Study of the Sociology of the Church* (Minneapolis: Fortress, 1998), 63.

5. Karl Barth, *Church Dogmatics* IV/2 (Edinburgh: T&T Clark, 1958), 818.

Chapter 3 The Breadth of Grace for the World

1. See L. Regnault, ed., *Les chemins de Dieu au désert: La collection systématique des apophtegmes des Pères* (Solesmes: Éditions de Solesmes, 2005), 340 (translation original).

2. Christoph Friedrich Blumhardt, *Action in Waiting* (New York: Plough, 2012), 30–31.

3. Owen Collins, ed., *2000 Years of Classic Christian Prayers: A Collection for Public and Personal Use* (London: HarperCollins, 1999), 51.

4. Karl Barth, *Fragments Grave and Gay*, ed. M. Rumscheidt (London: Collins Fortress Library, 1971), 45–46.

5. Karl Barth, *The Christian Life: Church Dogmatics* IV/4, *Lecture Fragments* (Edinburgh: T&T Clark, 1981), 80.

6. Barth, *Christian Life*, 80.

7. Martin Luther, *Luther's Works*, vol. 14, *Selected Psalms III*, ed. Jaroslav Pelikan and Daniel E. Poellot, trans. Arnold Guebert (St. Louis: Concordia, 1958), 163.

8. John Wesley, *The Works of John Wesley*, bicentennial edition, 35 vols. (Nashville: Abingdon, 1984), 1:280.

9. Wesley, *Works of John Wesley*, 1:281–82.

10. Wesley, *Works of John Wesley*, 1:274.

Conclusion

1. Excerpt from the hymn "And Can It Be?," *Singing the Faith* (London: Hymns Ancient and Modern, 2011), hymn 345.

Index

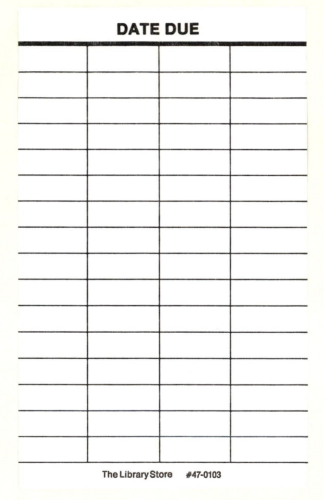

DATE DUE

The Library Store   #47-0103